The Art of Shopping

The Art of Shopping

*how we shop
and why we buy*

Siemon Scamell-Katz

LONDON   NEW YORK
MADRID   BARCELONA
MEXICO CITY   MONTERREY
BOGOTÁ   BUENOS AIRES

Published by
LID Publishing Ltd.
6-8 Underwood Street
London N1 7JQ (United Kingdom)
Ph. +44 (0)20 7831 8883
info@lidpublishing.com
LIDPUBLISHING.COM

A member of **B P R**
www.businesspublishersroundtable.com

Printed in Great Britain by T J International Ltd.

ISBN: 9781907794223
ISBN: 9781907794186
Collection editor: Jeanne Bracken
Cover design: Raúl Vázquez
Typesetting: SyS Alberquilla S.L.

First edition: April 2012

Contents

Contents

To Isy, Claudie and Foiy

Introduction

We were sitting around the wooden dining table that served as our meeting room table. We had watched all the video tapes. This was the first look at what the data was going to tell us. Rob had prepared a first print-out of the report.

I remember seeing arrows showing the flow of shoppers around the store, density maps highlighting the hot and cold spots in the store. Compared to the kind of data we produce today, it was almost laughably simple. At the time, however, it was ground-breaking. As we excitedly pored over the pages, we found ourselves grinning like fools at each other, realizing that this was a real breakthrough. Finally, we could measure what shoppers really did in-store. I actually felt that "itch" they talk about – and I knew that we had created something new, something big.

* * *

I first started working in shops when I was 16. The fiscal demands of my social life meant that a paper route was no longer enough; I needed a Saturday job. I had spent an afternoon window shopping with a girl that I fancied, thinking that this sacrifice would illustrate my ardour, and we visited Laura Ashley where she enthused about their merchandise. So I applied for a job there.

It is 1981. Picture a shy, skinny and awkward adolescent boy arriving for his first day of work. I am taken into the staff room to meet the store staff, about 20 girls aged 17 to 25, with an overwhelming scent of warmth, Laura Ashley cottons, cigarette smoke and about 20 conversations. I am in love. I toil, carrying boxes of tiles up three flights of stairs, spending hours tidying paint storerooms, stock-taking wallpaper borders, fetching and carrying for these deities. They all tease me, the Saturday girls the worst. One, a beautiful, crazy redhead, explains the meaning of love in one long, never-ending Saturday morning spent sorting paints: emulsion from gloss, colour from white. Slowly, I am released onto the shop floor where I discover a love for fabrics and patterns, colours and schemes. I am born into the Laura Ashley family and with it, my life's obsession with retail.

Partially because of the distracting nature of that social life, I mess up my A-level exams and shockingly find myself not at university discussing philosophy and left-wing politics in smoke-filled dorms, but instead, working in the back room of a bank in a tiny English market town. I spend a week keying the amounts written on all the cheques that have been paid to the branch into an Enigma-era computer. I spend days tearing statements from a huge pile, one by one, and putting them into envelopes. I spend weeks listening to the staff around me bitch about each other, the minutiae of their customers' lives, and no doubt me, too, when I am not there.

I lasted three months before I left and returned to Laura Ashley, this time as a management trainee. I worked in a stand-alone, soft-furnishing concession in a DIY store in my home town, and then moved away from home to another store as a junior manager (which meant I did the cashing up when nobody more senior was there to do it). Then, back to the ranks but this time to Regent Street, the firm's flagship store in London. This move took me from a shop with three staff to one with around 100, with special lines, visits from buyers and from the head office. It also brought Boxing Day sales with queues snaking down the street, as well as tourists – Americans buying armfuls of stuff, literally more than they can carry. I am young, and working and partying hard in central London. When I go and visit my friends at university, what am I missing?

The High Street revolution that is Next launches soon afterwards. After fashion comes Next Interior, much whispered about and soon they are recruiting for the launch. I land a job working in their refitted flagship store, again on Regent Street in London. This was a new retail concept from George Davies, the most talked-about retail revolutionary, and the work was about as high profile as High Street retailing gets. After a 110-hour work week we launched, first on press night and then we opened the doors to the public.

I worked in the Regent Street flagship store for about a year, migrating from soft furnishings to Next for Men and then, after a brief stint in the new espresso cafe (at the time, something of a novelty for a fashion store in London), I worked in the small, made-to-measure suits area of Next for Men.

I work hard and make friends with two "old-timers" from the Hepworth days (the retailer that Next rebranded). One, a Ugandan Asian, is the best salesman I have ever seen. I watch him sell a size 44" jacket to a guy that is at best, a 38". We also tailor the British Olympic team that year and, as a result, we sell a whole heap of extra suits. The other friend is a first generation Afro-Caribbean tailor with the best jazz-funk collection of LPs I've ever seen. Between the two of them, they taught me that a suit was not a jacket and trousers that came off a hanger, but cloth that could be crafted by artists to make a man look like a hero, no matter what his shape or size.

It is here that I stumble across marketing for the first time, without realizing it. Next ran a competition for all the branches with made-to-measure facilities, with a team prize for the highest increase in orders. In various sojourns to the stockrooms I remembered seeing box after box of what looked like tie boxes – but that in fact were the copies of the records of not only recent customers, but of customers going way back to the pre-Next days. I hit upon the idea of writing to all of these names and addresses and after typing out a standard letter, I handwrote the name and address of each of these contacts and persuaded the store manager to fund the postage. Miracle! We not only attracted a large number of lapsed customers to come back to the store to place orders for new suits, all clasping their letters, but we also won the competition.

This success, along with being the branch that the Next directors visited, led to an offer to go work at the head office. With two weeks' notice I moved from London to a bed and breakfast in Leicester run by a Scottish couple, both ex-ice skating dancers (who had a different tartan carpet on each floor).

Initially, I worked for Next Interior again, in customer services, and then came my big break. At the age of 21 I was accepted for the post of junior buyer and worked for the most inspirational boss I've ever had – John Miles. Recruited by George Davies from Royal College, John had a vision for Next Interior that was decades ahead of its time. He also had incredible energy and would frequently catch the train down to London to party all night and then be back, driving us on, first thing the next morning.

It was at this time that I was introduced to the world of design from a different point of view, meeting designers and manufacturers and working with them to create small batch run-offs of some great designs. Unfortunately, George Davies' star began to wane and after a breathtaking year of learning for me, Next Interior's buying was moved to Bradford to be managed by the net-curtain buyers of Grattan, the mail order firm that Next purchased. This meant that the Next Interior dream vanished, along with my job.

So, what next? The answer was simple: retail design. Somehow, unqualified as I was, I managed to get a job as a salesman with OYA, a recently-acquired part of the WPP empire, selling everything retail from store concepts through to point-of-sale fixtures. After a couple of years of frankly ineffective selling, I decided that I could do the job of running a design agency far more effectively. Together with three other employees we went through the drama of setting up a breakaway agency. I was 25, I had no idea what I was doing and no idea what a profit and loss account was. I soon learnt! As Ralph Waldo Emerson said, "Often a certain abdication of prudence and foresight creates an element of success". After a year, our dream agency was on the rocks (I still hadn't sold enough). We owed more than we had earned and the bank wasn't friends with us anymore. So we split the business in two and in return for reprieving a debt to the shopfitters, Antone, Andrew Freer and I set up ID Magasin, a new design agency where Paul Ransom (from the shopfitters) had 52 per cent and Andrew and I split the remainder of the shares.

It was a combination of two dreamers. We both approached any problem with the view that the standard approach to the answer was probably wrong, and that with some creative thinking a new approach or a better solution could be fashioned. We managed to persuade an audience that we were right: a very small audience who believed that a tiny new agency could fashion an approach to retail design from a different point of view. Given that we were in the depths of a vicious recession this was brave, but slowly, painfully slowly, we seemed to be breaking through. One client became two, and then through various stumbles we had three, at which point we decided to recruit. Paul Tirrell joined us to project manage and a really tall, lanky northerner called Rob Lawson, straight out of university, joined to help us think.

It was then that the story really started. We focused on the fact that we were designing stores and fixtures with no real conception of what shoppers actually *did*: where they went in the store, and once there, how they behaved. Every design agency, from large to small, was designing total shopfits down to free-standing promotional units with no idea at all about how it was going to work. It was, and still mainly is, an industry that relies on what things look like to sell the idea, rather than how it is going to work. Design awards are merited by agencies that produce good form; scant attention is given to function (ie, sales). It was a short journey from there to the discovery that the market research industry hadn't thought about this either. In fact, there were precious few techniques, aside from asking shoppers what they thought they had done, to answer the question. Frankly, we were amazed. How were finance directors making decisions about whether to roll out a shopfit, commission a re-layout of their stores or install fixtures and displays in the stores without knowing what impact it was going to have? We were talking about investment decisions in the region of millions of pounds and all that decided it was "it looks nice". Hmmmm.

Rob found that Roy Bradbury and Hugh Philips at Nottingham University had tried using still cameras to record and research shoppers' movements, so we hit on the idea of trying security video cameras to do the job – and shopper research as we know it today was born in the UK. Unknown to us, around the same time Herb Sorensen and Paco Underhill were starting in the US and previously, Georges Chetochine in France. Together, we are the godfathers of shopper research.

* * *

It has always been amazing to me that the creative industries are so conservative. Despite a veneer of fashion and innovation, creative industries are surprisingly backward-looking. In particular the marketing industry, along with the brands they serve and indeed the retailers that sell them, is almost ridiculously resistant to change. It would be laughable were it not that every one of us pays for this conservatism every time we buy a product.

Built-in failure is what we are paying for as consumers. Brands factor into their costs the research, design, advertising, promotion and listing fees that come with developing new products that consumers demand. Yet while consumers claim to want new products, the behaviour they display is different. According to Nielsen, the store sales monitoring agency, eight out of every ten new launches fail within three years.

So why are brands so complacent about this when their organizations are measured and motivated by their shareholders to be efficient in everything that they do? How is it that retailers, who fight like tigers for every cent and penny that they can squeeze out of brands, happily acquiesce to this cost of built-in failure?

The answer lies with another question: who would want change? Consumers are blissfully unaware that there is a massive industry constructed around this distressingly unsuccessful process, with new launches failing week after week after week. Consumers don't particularly want any change, and the vested interest of the whole industry rests on continuing with the dreadful norm, rather than with the opportunity for change.

Why does this failure happen? This is not some idiosyncratic, occasional process based on a brand manager's whim. Brands do not invest lightly in developing new products: they follow extremely planned processes and spend large amounts of management time and vast sums of money with agencies to develop tomorrow's winners. Despite this, tomorrow's winners are often yesterday's winners, as yet another line extension is launched and yet another "new" product benefit is ignored.

Part of the problem lies in the way the industry has developed, while another part is due to a fundamental absence of understanding the true motivation behind brand purchasing. People whose business this is simply fail to understand shoppers' motivations and behaviours; specifically, they either fail to clearly establish a need or to appreciate the way that products are bought in the store.

It is worth understanding a little of the gestation of a "new" product. Typically, a new idea comes from consumer research, either by investigating past purchasing patterns or by examining consumer lifestyles. Gaps are identified, most commonly within existing brand portfolios, sometimes in opportunities to create new brands, and very rarely to develop entirely new categories. Brands then work with strategic marketing or advertising agencies to "ideate" (develop the concept of) the new product.

Let's imagine an opportunity for a "new" toothpaste and say that research has identified that older consumers have different dental needs than younger ones; specifically, that older women (perhaps over age 50) have different cosmetic requirements to make their teeth appear whiter. A gap in the market for a new type of toothpaste then appears. Product developers and scientists either from inside or outside the business are given the task of creating this new product. The manufacturer's production teams are consulted and they start to plan ways in which existing machinery can be adapted or new machinery created to produce this new product.

A toothpaste that has special benefits for older, female consumers is then developed. The manufacturer and its strategic agencies will then consider whether they have an existing brand in their portfolio whose market position could extend to cover this new market. This approach is sensible, since an existing brand will already have clearly-established values in the minds of consumers. Existing advertising will have positioned the brand in a particular way, and the packaging for that brand will appeal to that market position. Let's imagine that our manufacturer has a brand that the marketers believe can stretch to accommodate the proposed positioning of the new product.

Several things will now happen. An advertising agency is briefed and asked to think of a creative idea that will communicate the brand's adapted position and the key product benefits. A packaging agency is briefed to take the design of the existing brand and create concepts that will adapt the "mother" brand to appeal to potential new consumers. After several iterations and client consultations the results of these two processes are given to a research agency. Concepts are tested both qualitatively and quantitatively to get feedback from consumers about the new product, the advertising and the package design. Other research agencies then ask consumers whether they would buy the new product and, depending on these responses, a financial model is then developed by the manufacturer. This establishes the size of the potential market as well as the volume and potential profit that would come from the new product's launch.

At each of these stages will be senior management sign-off, with many potential projects falling by the wayside if they fail to meet internal company benchmarks. Let's imagine that our intrepid new toothpaste has passed all these checks.

From those initial concept stages and early research will come changes and adaptations. As the manufacturer's production people get involved, compromises will have to be made about how the product is formulated and produced, how it is to be packaged and presented and how it will be packed.

Perhaps two years after the product is first imagined there will be samples that can be sent to the relevant regulatory bodies for testing to ensure that the product is safe, and to make sure that the product and packaging meets legislative requirements. Having passed that vital stage, the manufacturer is now ready to think about selling the product to retailers.

Beyond the market research that created the idea for the product and the concept testing that was part of its development, other research assesses how the new product will fit into the toothpaste category. For example, are there other products aimed at older consumers that could be grouped together with this new product? If the product succeeds, what impact will this have on the total category? Will it grow sales for the entire category? Where will this growth come from? What is the optimum price for the product so that it fairly reflects its brand position and product benefits?

Armed with all this information, the results of the tests and an idea of the likely publicity support (including advertising and PR), the product is then pitched to retailers. The retailers consider their own categories; their priority is to grow the total category. So how will this new product benefit the retailer? If it succeeds will it attract other manufacturers to produce a similar product? Is there an opportunity to create a private label version of this product? Other financial questions follow: what is the best margin that the retailer can get from the manufacturer? What payment terms can be negotiated? How much will the manufacturer pay to have the product put on the shelf? What kind of promotion is the manufacturer going to pay for to support the launch? Of course, many retailers make most of their profit (if not all of it) not from actually distributing and selling these products, but from what the manufacturer will pay them to sell it.

Our new brand then goes up for review alongside all the other product propositions from the manufacturer and their competitors. Ours is a great new idea, it's going to grow the entire category and the manufacturer has put down an appealing amount of money to pay the retailer to sell it, so we win! We get "listed".

We are now getting closer to launch. The supply chains for the retailer and the manufacturer estimate likely sales volumes and agree how they will ensure that the product is in stock for as much of the time as possible, based on projected sales. Another design agency is briefed on the launch displays that will be used to promote the product in-store. The advertising agency books time on television and space in newspapers and magazines. The PR agency launches the product with the relevant media, creating stories that the journalists can reprint in various trade and general publications.

The brand will probably design a facebook page, linking PR activity with social media sites. There will also be discussion about how to link the product into existing websites that discuss healthcare and beauty for older shoppers.

So, amid much noise and fanfare our new toothpaste is launched. Television ads run, stories of product benefits run in the press, displays show-off the product in the stores, and there is a major campaign targeted at dentists to promote the product in their surgeries – it is all systems go.

This is a pretty typical journey in the launch of a new brand. Thousands of people are involved in the product's creation and launch. For some of these people, this product has been the total focus of their working lives for the past two or three years. There has been massive investment in product development, sales and marketing. Yet despite the scope of this activity – the expertise employed and the investments made – most of this time and money will have been a total waste because most of these products will fail. And, just to be clear about where the bill goes, you are the one paying for this.

Why is this? Why does this process work so poorly?

There are three fundamental factors that will mean success or failure for any brand. These are important, whether the product is launching or during its lifecycle after its launch. The first issue is the product's *appeal*. Even if we are successful in making a potential consumer aware of the product, does it appeal? Does it meet some need or create some kind of desire in the mind of the consumer? The second issue can best be described as the product's *choosability*. Once a consumer gets to the store and becomes a shopper, do they see the product and choose to buy it? The final issue is one of *consumption.* When the shopper uses the product do they like it? Is it successful in meeting a specific want or need? The circle then repeats: do we want or need it enough to buy it again? Can we find it? Do we still like it compared to the alternatives? And so on.

Traditionally, the marketing industry has been very good at the first stage, understanding the consumer and making products look appealing, and also the last stage – making sure that the consumption process works. Surprisingly, it is only in the last 20 years that agencies like mine have focused on understanding the crucial second phase, what AG Lafley, until very recently CEO of Procter & Gamble, publicised as "The first moment of truth". If a product is not selected in-store, everything else described above is completely irrelevant. This book considers each of these stages but pays particular attention to the second one, the challenge of getting consumers to choose a product.

* * *

For years we struggled as we changed from being a retail design agency to a shopper research agency. The problem was that we were offering services that no one had ever thought about before, let alone bought. After using video in-store for the first time in the UK, we were later to become the first company in the world to use eye-tracking technology in-store. Working with Dr Mark Dunne from the Department of Vision Science at Aston University in the UK and two of his PhD students, we devised a study to measure the impact of presenting symbols either horizontally or vertically – a fundamental question when it comes to merchandising or laying out products on shelves. Next, we took the lab equipment and started to research in-store. I can remember taking the research proposal to Geoff Goode and Chris Cole at ITL and proposing research that we had little idea how to do, and no idea about the outcome. They were brave enough to try it and continued to support our early experiments. Slowly, we managed to sell the idea to a few more brands. Our second commercial breakthrough came when I went to see Chris Poole at Procter & Gamble. In the marketing world,

P&G and Unilever – two great, rival brand manufacturers – are the universities of marketing. Chris agreed to a project and once we had the endorsement of P&G as a client, new opportunities began to emerge.

A couple of times we nearly went out of business. Once we were hours away from having to close down, houses gone, etc. In that grim time Andrew and I parted ways. In one of the worst moments of my life to date, and in the interest of the survival of the business, I had to ask Andrew to leave, effectively firing my inspirational partner, mentor and friend. As a measure of the man's generosity he has since forgiven me.

We had been the first people in the UK to use video in-store and the first in the world to use eye-tracking in-store – the question was: what next? Working with Bob Stone at Salford University and the UK retailer the Co-op, we worked on the world's first virtual reality (VR) store, conducting the first ever retail research in VR. Other firsts followed: first to film an entire shopping trip in a superstore, first to use eye-tracking with fMRI brain scanning. Despite these new activities we found that the marketing world still wasn't really listening. So we asked Christine Kane at Campaign Marketing Services to help us promote our business. We would go to conferences and describe some of what we learned. Delegates loved what we had to say, but not too many put their hands in their pockets and bought our services! Then, slowly, our world started to change.

Several major brands recognized the importance of understanding shoppers as people who look and choose, and not simply as consumers who use. Our business grew and at one stage we employed around 60 people who were packed into three offices in Market Harborough, a small town in the UK Midlands. Marjorie Epson transformed us into a structured business, introducing the necessary systems and processes, and Tony Wren came in as finance director and together they got us onto an even keel – we became a proper business! We started to do more international work and we thought we must be successful because a succession of agencies started to copy our breakthrough methodologies and compete with us.

Eventually TNS, who were looking to invest in shopper research, bought my agency and that of one of my fellow pioneers, Herb Sorensen, in the US. This was followed by a shopper agency in China, Zdology. For all of us this was a fantastic opportunity: as small agencies, we could do country-level work, but rarely could we consider multi-country projects. For TNS, who have offices in 70 countries and are able to name just about every brand as a client, this was an opportunity to take our innovation to a global level.

Most investment in shopper research has been undertaken by the brands that are sold in supermarkets and most of what I intend to share with you in this book has come from that part of the retail world. We have studied millions of shoppers in most countries around the world, filming, eye-tracking and interviewing. We have also worked across every retail sector, so I will also discuss shoppers in some of the other major retail sectors such as fashion, variety, banks and department and big box stores such as DIY and Electrical.

In the past few years some of the greatest changes in the retail industry that I have seen in my working life have occurred. Our business, like shopping itself, is relentless and constantly changing. In this fascinating and exciting context, we continue pushing the boundaries of understanding so that we can help our clients function in a multi-channel world, both online and offline. Will we ever understand consumers and shoppers well enough? Probably not, but we're having a rollercoaster of a ride trying. Much has been achieved but there is still so much more to do.

1

Going to Market

"It has been said that man is a rational animal. All my life I have been searching for evidence which could support this."
Bertrand Russell

Occasionally I'm approached by journalists who ask about the secrets of supermarkets. What is it that they do to make us buy, even when we don't want to? What do they do to make us buy more? In the collective imagination there is a healthy suspicion that we are somehow being manipulated by malign forces, that we are being led, unwittingly, perhaps even hypnotically, to do things that we don't want to.

A hearty chuckle is my usual response. Twenty-first century retailing is a business that is highly sophisticated and in most countries, fiercely competitive, with each retailer watching their peers obsessively. One point that the best retailers have in common, without question, is the way they manage their supply chains. From buying products at the best price to getting them to the store and onto the shelf in the most efficient manner, the largest and most successful retailers have developed business models and supply chains that are widely recognized as world class.

Where most retailers are much less effective is in answering the question of what happens once those products are on the shelf, ready to be perused and bought. This is because many of the principles of retailing have evolved from unquestioned practices and been compounded by rumour and myth. This is only topped up by shoppers who when interviewed, give a partial, post-event rationalization for their actions. The simple truth is that while retailers may be fantastic at getting the product to the store, selling on the other hand, is not their speciality.

A vital aspect of great retailing should be successful marketing, and this is not a recent development. The earliest record of human farming is in Jericho, in the Middle East, around 10,000 years ago. At this time, mankind started to move from living a nomadic, hunter-gatherer existence into small farming groups where they began to grow crops. Villagers and farmers traded their excess products with other groups and crucially, farming also meant that one group in society could specialize in food production, allowing enough time for other members of that society to specialize and produce things other than food that could also be traded. Persuading people to exchange became the norm and that persuasion was the birth of marketing.

Taking a product to market is not only as old as civilization: it is also a fundamental component of trade. However, the means used to sell have become increasingly sophisticated. Despite this constant and steady evolution of marketing, it is only in the last 20 years that our understanding of *why* we buy has emerged by focusing on *how* we actually shop. The study of shopping marries science with art. Marketing any product is an activity at the mercy of the human condition and not every trend is always clear or quantifiable. While our decisions are rarely the product of cold, rational logic the use of the scientific method, based on observation, has been a revelation.

This is not to situate current debates on the history of marketing and retail as a mere development of medieval studies on the morality of economics. While pre-renaissance, ecclesiastical scholars concerned themselves more with the nature of a "just price" and the fairness of distribution, science has now enabled the exploration of the psychology of demand. Utility, previously the key to understanding how a product is sold, is increasingly redundant: we often pay for the idea of a product for complex psychological reasons, rather than for the product itself. "Need" has been overtaken by "want".

Between 1956 and 1963, *The Journal of Marketing* featured 23 biographical essays on the pioneers of marketing that proved seminal for two reasons. First, the rising consumption of the early 20th century produced a seismic increase in the professionalization of marketing. While some people and businesses instinctively understood the need to demonstrate customer focus, it was only after 1945 that the multiplication of advertising channels became seen as a way to enhance this and generate competitive advantage. In particular, the arrival of radio, television and cinema meant that this was now the age when a product's appeal could be cast more broadly than ever before: the age of broadcasting.

Second, marketing had evolved from being ignored or "bolted-on" to research and development, into a professional science. As with any "empire of the mind" the key is to stay ahead of the competition by seeking out the latest thinking. An example that demonstrates the importance of competition to marketing is the ban on tobacco advertising in much of the world. Surely if a firm's rivals are legally not permitted to advertise this is good for business chiefly because it is possible to save money without losing market share. What has happened in response, however, is an increasingly intensive search for new marketing tools that can be used in the fight for market share. This is actually the opposite of what has happened to most goods over the last century. Sectors such as film and fashion now sell products that are so de-commoditized that their production is considered an art form. The distinction between selling a product based on the benefits it offers and the self-image it can create is vital. Look at Apple.

A turning point in the history of marketing and retail came with the arrival of modern methods of statistical analysis. This enabled producers to dissect their selling environment. One of the leading statisticians was Ronald Fisher, a man who developed the study of variance and regression. This held the promise of allowing marketers to understand how variables such as demographics and sales were related so that marketing efforts could be focused. The development of a scientific language to enable marketers to analyse the marketplace created a paradigm shift in the behaviour of brands and consumers.

The art of retailing should be closely and inextricably linked with an understanding of shopping behaviour. With the arrival of supermarkets and the rapid economic growth after 1945 this evolved into a major, global business. In 1916, the first Piggly Wiggly store opened in Memphis, Tennessee and it was revolutionary because it was one of the first retailers to encourage self-service instead of employing clerks to bring goods from their warehouse to a customer at the counter. This approach encouraged shoppers to take a much more active role in deciding what to buy, rather than relying on the shopkeeper to sell. The first "real" supermarket was opened by Michael J. Cullen in 1930, inside a 6,000-square-foot (560 m²) former garage in Queens, New York City. Called "King Kullen", it used the slogan "Pile it high. Sell it low." At the time of Cullen's death in 1936 there were 17 King Kullen stores and the interaction between shopper and seller became transformed forever. All of this was followed by a long, slow demise of the practice of selling in shops, which was then replaced by the art of presenting a product in a space. That space ranged from spartan discount grocers to the most sumptuous clothing retailers.

To study the forces that influence shopping, one must recognize that the business of retailing is fundamentally different from that of a company like Boeing or Google. Shopping is about marketing a space where customers can spend. Gravity is essential to shopping, determining how individuals are drawn or repelled across the floor. Cullen's contribution was to create an area where shoppers could browse potentially unfamiliar products, rather than coming with predetermined needs and relying .on someone else to choose specific products for them. Just as Newton's Law of Gravitation led to a myriad of related concepts – impulse, inertia, force, etc – so the importance of space to shopping increased. A crucial point is that just as in physics, shoppers obey the law of entropy: understanding that they conserve momentum is the key to designing spaces that help them shop more effectively.

Observing and analyzing shopper behaviour is complicated by the fact that we as shoppers are consciously aware of only a fraction of our actions, so most of our decisions cannot be recalled. Since shopping is an art as much as a science, it is less important to develop predictive models "in theory" than it is to observe actual behaviour "in practice". In the seminal 1931 book *The Law of Retail Gravitation*, William J. Reilly acknowledged the decisive importance of space to the shopper, but as a "law" it is hard to extract predictive models. For instance, it seems perverse that "pick your own" strawberries are often more expensive than those in some supermarkets, or that Fair Trade coffee should be distinguished as a premium product when sitting on the shelves next to a relative abundance of cheaper alternatives. Such issues are a matter of taste and beliefs.

Formal advertising that influences these tastes and beliefs began towards the end of the 19th century, arriving in a world of visual simplicity and limited sources of information. This changed markedly with what Harold Wilson, then British Prime Minister, called the "white heat of technology" that arrived in the post-war years, with new sources of media creating new opportunities for advertising. Following the success of a serialized radio drama, *Ma Perkins*, in boosting sales of its sponsor, Procter Gamble's Oxydol detergent, other brands began to develop similar "soap operas". The first television advertisement was broadcast on July 1, 1941, when the watchmaker Bulova paid $9 for a placement before a baseball game. The 20-second spot displayed a picture of a clock superimposed over a map of the United States, accompanied by the voice-over "America runs on Bulova time". The model that has survived from the 1950s pushed for advertising to generate awareness of a product so as to gain market share.

There have often been flawed or misconceived techniques developed simply because people did not genuinely understand why shoppers and consumers were behaving in a particular way. For example, there is evidence of a disturbing disconnection in advertising theory between research and reality. An example of this was a 1999 soft drink television commercial featuring a bland, contemporary pop song. In focus groups, the target market, adolescents, repeatedly gave negative feedback to such an extent that it was recommended that the manufacturer pull the ad. Despite this advice they decided to go ahead and broadcast it anyway, and when they did, the ad was a resounding success and the drinks' market share exploded. Afterwards, the firm rationalized this unexpected result by arguing that the song's blandness actually benefited the ad, reassuring customers by conjuring images of routine, pleasant memories. This highlights the point that in marketing, what is important is often not the physical reality but how people process that reality and the context in which it is encountered.

Advertising attempts to be the modern continuation of salesmanship. It has brought a shift in the way that goods are marketed as seismic as the advent of the supermarket. Historically, advertising focuses on the consumer and even today, it uses outmoded models of linear persuasion: I get your attention, I stimulate your interest, I create desire, I therefore attain the purchase. However, it is the shopper that buys the product: money spent on helping people buy is critically different from money spent making people want to consume. In the same fashion, market research has come to focus less on what people recall thinking and more on how people feel, as advances in neurology have enabled the emotional state of the customer to be recorded.

In a vastly more complex and markedly less credulous marketplace than that of *Ma Perkins*, successful marketing makes an impact when it understands that there is a lack of selling in the retail space, and when it recognizes the limitations of what advertising can achieve. An understanding of how we shop has to be the starting point for how we consider the art of persuasion. The next chapter highlights some of the most significant insights from our research into the way that people actually shop – information that is slowly shifting the thinking of some retailers and brands. It explains how people around the world approach this vital, mundane task, describes their typical mindset and introduces the crucial notion of shopping *missions*.

2

Going Shopping

"A person buying ordinary products in a supermarket
is in touch with his deepest emotions."
JK Galbraith

How do you go shopping? You may not realize it but about eight people out of ten choose to use the same store for their food shopping. This is true wherever you go in the world. It occurs despite the fact that in many places, especially the developed countries of Europe and North America, there is a large choice of modern retailers and store formats, all within close proximity of people's homes and workplaces. This simple truth hints at a much larger issue: the influence of mindset and behaviour when deciding where to shop. The question is: why should this be? How do we choose one store over others? What makes us use the same store again and again – is it just down to pricing?

As it turns out, pricing is not the most significant issue at all. While most shoppers have a pretty accurate view of the typical cost of shopping with their chosen retailer (and a perception of the cost of a similar basket in the other retailers), it is not the most common reason why shoppers choose outlets. This is because large, modern trade retailers (such as Walmart, Carrefour and Tesco) all tend to target a similar mass-market group with similar offerings. So while shoppers may decide to rank retailers by the likely cost of a weekly shopping trip, because there is only a small difference, other factors come into play.

In fact, the most important factor when determining the choice of a shop is location. People prefer the store that is nearest to their homes or on their journey from work, for example. This choice based on location also reflects how individuals view the process of going grocery shopping and how it fits into their lives. In the broader discussion about cost and depending on the relative importance of money and time to each of us, the more we prioritise one over the other in our choice of a shopping location. As an illustration of the importance of location consider the German-owned drugstore chain called Rossman. They moved one of their stores in the Czech Republic 150m along the same road. The initial store was next to a bus stop going out of town. The new location was next to a bus stop going into town. Store sales increased by 36 per cent simply by moving to a location that better suited shoppers.

We mostly see the weekly, home-replenishment shopping trip as a chore, something to be squeezed around other, more important, things in our lives. This means that the choice of store is in itself a function of lifestyle. If I am a 25-year-old single male in London I may well shop in a couple of small convenience retailers; one may be adjacent to the tube station that I use to go to and from work and one on a social route (perhaps to a gym or restaurant) – here I absolutely prioritise time cost over fiscal cost. If I am a non-working mother in Germany, I will probably use a store that is along the route to my children's school, and if I am pensioner in the townships of Johannesburg I will use the Spaza shop run out of a neighbour's garage and a supermarket that is on the bus route.

So the other factor that informs the choice of store is time. The busy young, single male in London may be working long hours and will only invest a very limited amount of time to the functional process of shopping, something that a small convenience store can deliver. The German housewife will probably do a big shopping trip and buy most of her groceries once a week, probably on the same day each week as it fits with her schedule. Although she may regard food shopping as a chore rather than a pleasure, a big weekly shopping excursion is more time efficient and means she will not feel particularly pressured (unless accompanied by a small child!). For our South African pensioner there are very few time pressures and going shopping will be a major part of their social interaction with the community – here I accept the cost of time to achieve a better fiscal benefit. The daily visit to the Spaza store, where news is exchanged, is the hub of the community in much the same way that a church would have been to a European during the Middle Ages.

It's also worth nothing that for very low income shoppers in developed markets, lack of access to transport means that they often have little choice but to use convenience shops. These low income areas, notable for their lack of choice in stores for shopping, are referred to as "food deserts". This lack of income and choice is made even worse by the fact that the convenience stores are generally more expensive than the large, inaccessible, out-of-town stores and also tend to provide little, if any, fresh produce.

So it is not necessarily price that drives the shopper's choice in many developed countries, but how the location of that store fits into their lifestyle. Proof of this is seen in the continuing growth of convenience stores where higher prices are accepted because a visit to the store fits more easily into a busy lifestyle. In contrast, the Johannesburg pensioner pores over the supermarkets advertising flyers to compare prices of staple items and it is this that drives the choice of store, within the limits of available transport.

In developed countries most of us use several stores. Perhaps one for a big weekly shop and another for smaller shop visits made either to replace fresh products or to respond to a change of plan for eating during the week. Recognizing these differing shopping styles or "missions" has had a dramatic impact on retailer thinking since the end of the 1990s – and not just when it comes to buying food. Shopping missions are the response to a shopping need and should be considered in every retailer's strategy. You may go shopping for a little black dress for a party tonight or you may just be browsing, looking for inspiration. You visit the same store for both of these missions, but how you use the store is different because of your shopping mission.

It's possible you may be shopping for a washing machine and are on a mission to research various options. Once you have decided on the model to buy, the next visit to the same store will be different. The retailer has to plan for every mission and decide which ones to focus on. The choice of store for the first mission will be the one that has a large range of options so that you can start to narrow down from what is available. Perhaps you also want to inspect a few models that you saw online. You may want to talk to a member of the sales staff for advice and explanations of the main features. That is why shoppers will often go to small independent retailers first for trustworthy advice and later, once the product choice is narrowed down, to the large, out-of-town retailers who are perceived to have better prices. Different missions demand different requirements from the stores.

Since the 1970s there has been a steady consolidation of market share by a few retailers in the developed markets of Europe and North America. This trend originated in North America and led to stores becoming larger and larger. Often, a very large store would open on the edge of town (or even out of town, where property was cheaper) and compete against smaller supermarkets located in the centres of several nearby towns.

The combination of having a reputation for low prices with an ability to offer not only food but a wide range of other products (from clothes to televisions and financial services) meant that small supermarkets began to close. This was a better business model for the retailer as it led to lower operating costs – as companies only had to deliver to a few large stores rather than many smaller ones and they needed fewer employees overall. In the town in the UK where I grew up in the 1970s there were two small supermarkets, one "International" supermarket (of about 6,000 square feet) and the other a "Safeway" (around 10,000 square feet). Twenty years later those two retailers have gone out of business and been replaced by a 60,000-square-foot Tesco store. This consolidation among retailers together with continued reliance on advertising to sell has led to many stores effectively becoming warehouses – places where we go simply to collect our purchases, not necessarily choose them.

With a growing interest in missions and a desire to understand how shoppers used their stores, we were asked by one of the top two UK grocery chains to investigate how the layout of their stores worked. In particular: how did shoppers enter and move around the store; did the order of the categories in the store match the way that shoppers used them? This was a breakthrough project: previously, most of the research had been focused on categories and been funded by manufacturers rather than retailers. We decided to conduct the research in a large supermarket on the edge of Bristol. We proposed to the retailer that we would install 120 small cameras in the ceiling of the store wired to a control suite. Using all 120 cameras, a camera operator who was based in a storeroom, would track shoppers as they came into the store and then record their journeys. We planned to do this every day for four weeks and film 400 shoppers at different times of the day and week. Lastly, as shoppers left the store one of our interviewers would approach the shopper and ask questions about the frequency of their store visits and how successfully the store satisfied their needs. The VHS recordings were sent back to our offices and our team of watchers drew each shopper's journey around the store on a paper store plan. They recorded where the shoppers stopped, where they started and finished their shopping and how long they took, along with a myriad of other measurements that we commonly use when filming shoppers. This required a team of 21 people watching for 12 hours each day which came to a total of over 5,000 hours of watching those 400 shoppers. The data from the films was combined with information from each respondent's interview.

What did we find? Around one-third of the shoppers shopped two or three times a week at the store, a further one-third used the store once a week and around two-thirds identified the supermarket as their main store for food shopping. The majority of shoppers were usually very familiar with the store. The retailer had asked us to look at the two biggest missions: the *main shop* where the shopper was buying most of the groceries needed for the next week and the *top up* where the shopper was buying things in addition to the main shop.

This was when we made a startling discovery. The large supermarket had been designed to suit the "typical" shopper, and in its design it was very similar to thousands of supermarkets around the world. The designers pictured a 35-year-old mother of two children, shopping with a trolley and doing the weekly shopping for the family. They had the wrong person. Two-thirds of the shoppers in the store were making top-up shopping trips. The immediate consequence of this was that most of their customers were faced with the inconvenience of having to trek around dozens of grocery aisles to buy only a few products. This often proved to be a difficult and needlessly time consuming task. So, while the bakery was at the back of the store and was perfectly convenient for the main shopper, someone on a top-up mission had to cross one-third of the store to get bread, followed by another hike to get milk and all before standing behind a shopper with a packed trolley for ten minutes at the checkout. This was reflected in how long the shoppers spent in the store. The main shopper was buying around 50 items and taking 38 minutes, whereas the top-up shopper, buying just 15 items or less, was taking 22 minutes. Many customers were having their lives made more difficult. This cash-rich, time-poor population was rushing around and coping with the supermarket, not valuing it.

While the two groups' most popular categories were identical (for example, fresh produce, meats, bread and milk), the shoppers' mindset and the way they behaved on the two missions was different. We saw that shoppers doing a main shop were far more likely to interact with promotions and to comprehensively approach most aisles in a systematic fashion. The main shopper tended to snake up and down the first few aisles and then skip some aisles, snake again for a couple of aisles while working their way along the top part of the store and returning along a part of the bottom area of the store before heading for the checkouts. Top-up shoppers tended to make greater use of the middle-cross break (the big access aisle that runs the width of the store) or pass along the top break (the access aisle at the top perimeter of the store), dipping in, u-turning and coming out of the aisle.

To improve their targeting of different customers, the retailer would need to adjust the layout of the store to match the shopper's psychology. In short, the mission drove the mindset of the shopper – from the actual store they chose to how they used it and whether they found it an experience they would be keen on repeating. Of course, the same shopper could complete different missions at the same store during the same week. This meant that our main shoppers were not necessarily a different group of people than the top-up shoppers, just that they behaved differently depending on the mission that they had set themselves.

Later, we interviewed several shoppers on film and asked them to describe their different shopping missions. Our first film featured Linda, a mother of two teenage children, and opened with her at home, checking cupboards and formulating the shopping list with her family during the week. She arrived at the supermarket and her initial decisions were focused around the meals she planned to make over the coming days and the ingredients she would need.

While her list comprised only about ten items, the store provided her with a reminder for additional categories that she needed. In some categories, she encountered promotions for certain brands that affected her decisions. For example, she swapped chilled pizzas which were reasonably priced, for frozen pizzas at an even better price. Linda saw a promotion for a shampoo that she thought was a very good offer, but it was for a brand that she didn't buy, so she didn't take up the offer. After the early meal-building exercise, she switched to replenishing the stock cupboard, replacing those categories that she either bought on a weekly basis (for example, cereal) that were not on the list, or less regular purchases (such as household cleaning items) that were. She then completed her purchases with a couple of treats for herself from the personal care category. The whole exercise took about an hour and involved a mixture of routine behaviour in most categories and some browsing in a few categories.

Next, we watched Olivia, a young marketer, who was in the same supermarket buying food after work for a meal that evening. She had written a short list during the day and she dipped around the store putting those few pre-planned food items into her basket. Her priority was to get her shopping done quickly as she was tired after her day at work. She ignored any categories that were irrelevant and also any promotions. She went to the self-service checkouts, again with the aim of completing the shopping as quickly as possible, but mentioned that she would be coming back at the weekend to do her main shop.

Then there was Tracey, a new mum going to her first day at work and on the way, dropping off her daughter Ruth at the nursery. While packing her baby's bag, Tracey discovered that she had nearly run out of nappies and so had to factor in a visit to a store on the way to work. She chose the convenience store so that she could park directly outside and dash in, with her baby Ruth, straight to the nappies shelf. There she picked up the only brand available, went straight to the till, paid and left the store. All of this happened so quickly that she was able to drop Ruth off at the nursery and get to her new job on time.

For all three of our shoppers, the task had set the mission, which in turn determined the store they used and the way they shopped. This ranged from a mixture of browsing and promotion-seeking for one shopper, Linda, to a targeted rush resembling a cruise missile strike for Tracey, who just wanted to go into the store, buy one product and get right back out.

Following on from this groundbreaking project, we continued to research shopping missions. We began to understand that in the developed world's hypermarkets and supermarkets there were at least five general types of shopping trips, while in convenience stores there could be up to 12 missions. Sometimes, there were factors specific to a particular country that resulted in idiosyncratic behaviour. For example, in the US we discovered a *monthly* shopping mission, driven by the fact that shoppers had both large cars and large houses with ample storage, allowing them to make enormous "bulk buys". In Russia, supermarket buying is relatively novel, as many customers were still migrating from their previous habit of buying at fresh, daily markets. So we saw many large stores being used much more regularly, with a real focus on fresh food and people enjoying the novelty. In Vietnam, where the main mode of transport is the scooter or motorbike, shoppers could not buy in bulk so they would shop daily for amounts that could be carried on a bike.

The projects we completed identified two major issues. First, retailers must adapt their stores to cater to many different types of customers, each with different needs. The wide range of shoppers' differing demands has to be reflected in the stores' layout, promotions, merchandising (the way that products are displayed on the shelf), assortment (the range they carry) and pricing.

The second issue we identified is the need for manufacturers to respond to the same challenges and cater to diverse customers. For instance, do they manufacture a package size suitable for a big monthly purchase in the US? Do they manufacture a hair product size suitable for a daily purchase in Nigeria, where the shopper perhaps couldn't afford to buy a whole multiple-use pack at once? Our research highlights that our understanding of shopping has undergone a transition from a single dimension to a vastly more complex, multi-dimensional one.

In some places, both in developed and emerging countries, we are seeing a growth in small, "basket only" shops. This is noticeable where a lot of people live in small dwellings with limited storage, such as in high-density urban areas like New York, London and Moscow. Also, changing family structures, with more and more single households arising as a result of falling marriage rates and an ageing population, have deeply impacted shopping behaviour. Consequently, more people are using the shop itself as their larder and following a "just-in-time" principle, with products bought on the day they are needed. While this reduces wastage, it makes irregularity in shopping behaviour far harder for retailers to manage.

This increased frequency of shopping appears to have reduced the amount of wastage by households but, even so, a shocking 15 per cent of the food that UK shoppers buy is still thrown out. Often, single households find that there are simply no packs that are suitable for them and as a result, they are buying more than they need. Also, paychecks and size of dwellings play important roles. For example, the pension, which is the main source of income for many households in South Africa, is paid monthly and therefore determines when shoppers go to buy their staples. Canadian shoppers tend to have two freezers and basement storage facilities so like Americans, they tend to shop monthly.

Through the boom times of the 1990s, consumers in Europe and North America went shopping more and more frequently. However, in response to times of economic hardship, for example from 2008 onwards, we see shoppers reducing the number of missions that they do in a week in some countries. Instead, shoppers are conducting more organized weekly shopping trips, whereas in other countries we see shoppers shopping every couple of days which means they are just buying what they need to eat now. So whereas you typically see only around one-third of shoppers using lists, this proportion grows as shoppers try to plan more effectively. They also reduce the amount of times that they drop by a store to do a less-organized top-up shop, which means they can avoid stores that are more expensive and buying from categories that they hadn't planned on.

Sometime after our first research into missions, we began discussions with Waitrose, an upmarket grocer that operates small supermarkets in relatively affluent areas of the UK. They had recently recruited the most experienced store design director in Europe, Diana Hunter, to help develop their thinking about their stores and how well they reflected customers' needs. By this time (the 2000s) major retailers were no longer thinking only about those big stores lurking on the edge of town and closing down smaller stores. Most retailers had responded to the new realization of "missions" and were opening stores with different formats. There were small convenience stores in forecourts and in local neighbourhoods, small supermarkets on town High Streets, large supermarkets on the edges of towns and hypermarkets in big, out-of-town retail parks. However, while smaller and more flexible stores were increasing in popularity, they still suffered from difficulties in creating multi-mission spaces.

Diana suggested we visit some of the Waitrose stores and conduct a review, applying the lessons of our research to the current Waitrose concept. The report wasn't positive. The Waitrose product was fantastic and their shoppers loved the Waitrose brand, but their stores were not the best at helping their customers to shop.

It was agreed that we would look at their most typical supermarket format, about 25,000 square feet of retail space, and a store in Newbury about 50 miles west of London was chosen. We repeated the methods used previously, installing cameras and tracking 1,000 shoppers over four weeks. Our conclusion was that there were four main types of shopping missions and that the Waitrose layout was ineffective. We suggested that their layout was restricting sales and developed an idea for reorganizing the space that Diana asked us to present to the board. Our presentation received a rather shocked reception. When interviewed, Waitrose shoppers indicated that the stores were fantastic. However, this was not what we saw on our film, which indicated that they were being inconvenienced. So what created the disparity between what shoppers said and their actual behaviour on video?

Deciding to investigate further, we reviewed three other Waitrose stores using the same methods, filming and interviewing a representative sample. We discovered the same issues were common to all of the stores. Finally, Diana and I sat down with the managing director and presented our recommendations. The managing director was still sceptical but admitted that filmed evidence was difficult to argue against, and agreed that Diana should use the findings to develop a new store layout. In a radical effort, the new layout created several routes around the store to facilitate a number of different types of missions, rather than only catering to one "average" type of customer. This became the first truly multi-mission store in the world.

It was a great success. Sales boomed, shoppers shopped more frequently and they loved their store even more. Crucially, we had proven that a multi-mission store could thrive and that we could also increase customer loyalty without relying on expensive promotions. We simply needed to create an environment that matched what the shoppers were trying to accomplish.

Around the same time we also began working with Unilever to develop an optimal convenience store. In partnership with United Co-op and with a great project team we again went through the process of installing cameras and filming and interviewing shoppers in a small convenience store in the UK Midlands. Again we identified the different missions that were happening in the stores and the various ways that people behaved on each mission. This time we also pioneered the use of virtual reality (VR). Working with another agency that built the original store in a virtual reality computer model form, we asked shoppers to shop in the original layout. We then had the new layout created in virtual reality and asked shoppers to shop the new store layout.

The findings were promising. Following a refit of the original store we tested the new layout that the VR trial had suggested was optimal. Again, the cameras were used and we waited to see the results of the recommendations. Just about every category in the store was improved and attracted more shoppers. The flow around the store was more efficient and we found shoppers using the store more frequently and for more missions. Sales increased enormously. United Co-op rolled out the concept to several more stores with the same results: sales increased in all the outlets. Again, a multi-mission design was making shopping more efficient and encouraging shoppers to be more loyal to the store.

Of course, loyalty is a vital element of any retailer's future. This is especially true in countries where there is retail saturation, with more than one retailer available to each shopper. In these markets, the competition is fierce both to recruit shoppers from other retailers and to retain them once they start shopping with you. Hence the perennial price wars. Interestingly, while loyalty cards have a role to play in determining market share they are, perhaps surprisingly, not that influential on store choice. Research completed in the late 1990s by a major manufacturer showed that the average European shopper had loyalty cards for at least two retailers in their wallet, and would frequently buy from other vendors anyway. In any case, the chief function of a loyalty card is to provide useful data about shoppers' buying behaviour, and not, as the name would suggest, to reward loyalty.

As the discovery of shopping missions suggests, the answer to the question, "How do you go shopping?" is surprisingly complex and varied. In poorer countries, price is much more important in determining a retailer's success. As we mentioned earlier, a typical shopper in a South African township tends to make much greater use of price advertising than a more affluent customer.

Also, as time becomes more valuable to customers, it is even more important for the shop to be intelligently laid out, with the design of the space incorporating an awareness of the variety of shopping missions. The development of different store formats is designed to maintain loyalty in different ways and for different needs – such as Carrefour's franchises in France that include full service supermarkets, click and collect outlets (order online, collect from a warehouse), hypermarkets and convenience stores.

Another hugely-significant issue, alongside time efficiency, is the retailer's *brand positioning*. Some retailers, like Whole Foods in the US, have focused strongly on developing a strong quality and environmentally-responsible position and this is reflected in the way they display products within their stores. For example, reflecting an impressive attention to detail, staff are briefed to display peppers with the "stalk out" towards the shopper. Retailers like Tesco have also worked hard to develop quality positioning, with the result that most shoppers now believe their own brand products to be as good as, if not better than, manufacturers' brands. Publix, again in the US, has focused on developing a strong emotional relationship with their shoppers through advertising, focusing on the emotive relationships within the family and how Publix has a role in facilitating these. If you have children, I challenge you to watch their Valentine's Day ads without shedding a tear. Issues of branding, advertising and consumers' perceptions are clearly important influences on the way we shop, providing a further source of competitive advantage for those retailers that get it right. We discuss these issues in more detail later, particularly in Chapter Ten (Creating Appeal and Establishing Memories).

Understanding the complex nature of missions is particularly relevant for manufacturers too. If most of the people buying from your category are in the convenience store on a distress purchase – that is, they have run out of stock at home and all they want is a small emergency pack – then they are much less likely to buy the family size. This is especially true if the convenience store is perceived as charging higher prices. This means that manufacturers can create assortments of products that match the missions and motivations of the shopper, not only in terms of how they shop overall in the store but also how they shop in each category.

Furthermore, a mission-based assortment of products gives shops the flexibility to adjust the range of stock or inventory that they carry, with three valuable benefits: the retailer reduces their capital tied up in stock, they reduce the cost of unnecessary distribution, and there is a reduced but clearly-targeted assortment of products that increase sales. This is because the shopper can actually see what there is among all the choice and that makes buying decisions far easier.

As a result of this work, manufacturers also started working more intensively with the concept of shopping "missions". Coca-Cola invited us to study the way that different shopping missions in supermarkets influenced the sale of soft drinks, with interesting results. After researching the sector, we concluded that soft drinks, previously considered to be an impulse purchase by both soft drinks manufacturers and retailers, were in fact often a staple component of regular shopping trips. Shoppers were replenishing the stock of the product held at home, rather than grabbing a can or bottle on impulse. Consequently, most of the shoppers in supermarkets and hypermarkets came to the soft drinks section not because of a random walk or even a one-time promotion but because of planning: they were on a main shopping mission. In fact, the soft drinks category turned out to be one of the most heavily planned in the whole store. Given that only around 30 per cent of the people in the store were conducting a main shop, Coca-Cola realized that 70 per cent of shoppers were not only *not* buying from this category, they weren't even entering the aisle where their products were sold.

Coca-Cola's response was to reconsider both the package sizes and the locations where they were sold. In many stores in the UK there is a lunchtime mission, even in out-of-town stores, where shoppers come to buy drinks and sandwiches for lunch. Coke worked with the retailers to develop a lunchtime fixture with a chilled, immediate-use range. Coke also looked at how the product was used in the home and whether people stocked up on it after they had run out, or whether they replenished stock just before running out. This meant that in the main soft drinks aisle they could supply the best sizes to match home consumption. They also examined where the top-up shoppers that didn't come into the soft drinks aisle went in the store, and used this information to find other opportunities to place soft drinks products, for example, with crisps and snacks products.

While grocery retailers and manufacturers have been working with the idea of shopping missions for over a decade with notable success, many other retailer sectors do not even consider it when designing their stores. Consider, for example, mobile or cell phone retailing, one of the fastest growing retail sectors. The design of the store, wherever it is located and whatever the brand, is very similar. You will see a row of products around the store, usually on the walls, with some consultation areas and staff floating around. The environment is not at all adapted to the different missions of research, refinement of choice and purchase, and this is why shoppers so often start shopping with one brand in mind and end up completing their purchase with another. The stores are not designed for selling.

This reflects a fundamental weakness of the retail design industry. Shops are designed to look good but without a detailed understanding of how shoppers actually shop. Amazingly, given the cost of fitting a store, most decisions about store design are made with a minimum of shopper response or simply by asking a group of shoppers "Whether they like it" to whether they "like it". From the most expensive and exclusive fashion outlets to the hard discounter, a lack of understanding about how shoppers shop for clothes makes the goal harder than is necessary both for retailers and shoppers. It means that incredibly, one in ten shoppers who enter a fashion store intending to buy a product walk out because they couldn't find it – *even though it was there!* If you are a retailer, it is certainly worth asking what the different shopping missions are in your stores. What are the most important missions? How do shoppers look at products on these different missions? How can shoppers be motivated to go from looking at a product to picking it up, and then what is the best way to close the sale?

What is startling is that most retailers cannot definitively answer any of these questions. This fact is explored in the next chapter, which explains what happens when we arrive at a shop, the impact of signage, and where our attention is typically focused.

3

Through The Looking Glass

"Sometimes I've believed as many as six
impossible things before breakfast."
Lewis Carroll

The arrangement of window displays has long been recognized as an important part of good retailing. As far back as 1883 the classic book *A Guide to Window-Dressing* underlined the importance of creating a good first impression. Today, shoppers talk about "going window shopping" and a good window display entices shoppers to come into the store. Also, talk to most store managers of a High Street store and they will tell you that putting something on display in the window will guarantee an increase in sales for that particular item.

I was certainly aware of the window display's significance when, after a year spent working for UK fashion retailer Laura Ashley, I was asked to dress the window. This felt like a recognition of success since a great deal of emphasis was put on getting the window right. I remember spending a day arranging products in the window, then walking out onto the street and looking at it from across the road before returning to improve the position of a particular product. Later, as part of the buying team at Next, a retailer who took great pride in their window displays, we were posed with a further problem: how to deal with different stores in a large chain having widely different abilities at arranging their displays? The solution lay with the head office, where a window dresser would dress the window in a mock shop built on the ground floor; this would then be photographed and sent out to every store so they could copy the layout and ensure a consistent approach. Area managers, as part of their visits to stores, would take into consideration the quality of window treatments as one of their measures of success, and the imminent arrival of the area manager would have us running around titivating to ensure that we would receive a good appraisal.

Having had the importance of window displays drummed into me as a youngster, it seemed sensible to find out the science behind this shopkeepers' principle. When dressing a window in the way I had learnt at Laura Ashley, emphasis is placed on "front elevation". In other words, we stand back from the window and look at the window head on. However, this practice was revolutionized by research conducted with Dorothy Perkins, the UK-based women's fashion retailer, using eye-tracking technology. Eye-tracking gives us the ability to see what the shopper is seeing, through an adapted pair of glasses that we ask the shopper to wear. A tiny video camera mounted on the frame of the glasses not only records their field of view, but also shows which objects they focus on and for how long, by using an infrared beam that is projected into the eye and tracks the movement of the cornea.

As with the video footage of shoppers walking around stores we also watch this footage, albeit much more slowly, frame by frame. It takes us around ten hours to watch one person shopping for four to five minutes. The purpose of eye tracking is to see exactly what the shopper looked at so we can understand what attracted their attention, what might have influenced a decision, precisely how and when they reacted to different elements of the window and the layout of products – and what makes them buy.

We recruited 30 shoppers and asked them to walk along the High Street and go shopping in a Dorothy Perkins store. Then, after they had finished shopping, we interviewed them to find out what they could remember doing and seeing. As part of the interview we showed them the film of their eye movements and used that as a prompt to further explore some of the navigational and interaction decisions they had made. We also interviewed other shoppers as they left the store to understand why they had gone shopping there and what they could remember seeing.

When we started to analyse the footage several surprising and challenging facts were revealed. We found that windows were rarely viewed "square on" as shoppers walked along the High Street, as shopkeepers expected, because of the angle of approach. Shoppers tend to walk alongside windows, which limits their view to a very narrow angle. Only a tiny fraction of the whole window potentially affects their potential decision to enter. Moreover, the majority of shoppers ignored the windows entirely, concentrating their attention on the doorway. From our exit interviews, most shoppers did not recall a single detail of the window displays. The most detailed response from those who could recall them was, "I remember a brown dress in the window". This seemed to challenge all the long-held wisdom about the role of windows in driving traffic into the store.

To investigate further, we put cameras in the store windows facing outwards and filmed shoppers as they were passing by. We counted 9,108 shoppers over nearly three weeks and the results reinforced what had been suggested by eye tracking. Only 8–10 per cent of pedestrians looked at the store at all as they passed. Of these, the vast majority looked in through the door, rather than at the windows, suggesting that the most important area of the exterior was not the windows, or indeed the fascia board where the store name was (from what eye-tracking showed us, nobody had looked at this at all), but the view through the door. No relationship could be established between looking at the window and entering the store. In addition, the oblique angle of approach meant that most of the window's views were noticed by people who had already decided to enter. Incredibly, despite the fact that very few shoppers were looking at the window before they entered, when they were interviewed upon leaving, one-third of shoppers claimed that they *had* spent time looking at the window first – even though this was false!

This is a behaviour that we have seen many times since. People may not be able to remember what they have done but crucially, they have a perception of how they shop. This means that when they are asked about their shopping behaviour they post-rationalize their experience instead, and say what they *expect* they have done. This is the source of many of the myths of retailing. In fact, many of the things that manufacturers and retailers do are based on what people claim they do, rather than on what they *actually* do. Our perceptions about how we behave and our self-expectations of rational, logical behaviour direct what we think we have done. This situation is reinforced by the fact that shopping, like many things we do in life, is done unconsciously; so when an interviewer asks us to explain what we have done, we report an expected behaviour, not an actual one.

For example, we know that retailers use shop windows to entice us into their stores. The phrase "window shopping" is part of the lexicon describing what people do when they go shopping, therefore windows must be used. In fact, in most High Streets and shopping malls, fewer than five per cent of people window shop. Retailers simply listen to this claimed behaviour and the whole thing becomes a self-fulfilling fantasy, and serious money is spent on these fantasies.

What about the fascia that advertises the shop name? From working in store design, I recall that communicating a corporate identity was seen as absolutely vital. So much so, it would typically cost thousands of pounds to design and install. Yet the study highlighted that shoppers never look at it! Despite all the resources devoted to fascias and windows they play little or no role in attracting shoppers into the store.

Later we conducted research for Guinness in Dublin, Ireland. They devoted significant resources to installing Guinness "bus stop" signs outside just about every pub in the city. Clearly the idea was that with around half of pub visitors yet to decide on what they were going to drink when they got to the pub, the advertising sign outside would provide a timely reminder as they headed to the bar to order. The logic is compelling, but again we discovered that most shoppers didn't look at the sign at all, and if they did, all it communicated to them was that this was a location of a pub. It did not influence their choice of drink once they arrived. Guinness debated about whether to stop installing the signs, but decided in the end that the signs did have a role: not for the people entering the bars but simply for advertising the Guinness brand to those passing by on buses and in cars.

Unilever, one of the biggest food, drink and beauty companies in the world, spends millions of dollars every year on advertising. One part of this budget is for advertising outside supermarkets: on A-frames, posters and around the stores' car parks. Perhaps unsurprisingly, retailers charge significant sums for these locations: they are a good source of income. So every week printers are busy producing posters that are sent out to the store, and staff spend time putting out the posters and other dressings that have been supplied to them. Working with the media-planning agency that bought this advertising space on Unilever's behalf, we again used eye-tracking research from the car parks of two supermarket retailers and a convenience store chain to gauge the effectiveness of this advertising. Again, the return on this investment was extremely limited. As the shopper entered the car park, their attention was focused on the shopping mission at hand, together with the immediate challenge of locating a basket or trolley. They also had to be aware of moving traffic and mentally check their bags and wallets. Most of this activity was unconscious, but it meant that even for the very few shoppers who actually looked at Unilever's expensive posters, little of the information was noted and the effect on sales revenue was negligible.

Similarly, we also looked at the window dressings that the UK lottery company Camelot used in convenience stores to advertise the UK national lottery. Yet again, nobody looked at the windows before going into the outlet. Camelot then took the bold decision to use their point-of-sale (POS) material budget more effectively, and decided to stop putting displays in windows. When this was announced at the annual sales conference there was a near riot. A concerned salesforce thought the decision was mad! Quite reasonably, they believed that removing POS would kill the sales of the lottery. Despite this concern, the firm went ahead and cancelled all window treatments – with zero effect on sales.

We have seen this again and again: for fashion retailers, banks, fast-food restaurants, convenience stores and others. Store windows, instead of being directly involved in enticing passers-by to come in, appear to be effectively outdoor advertising, like a poster on the side of a bus.

So, what is happening? Most of us shop in the same, familiar High Streets and we learn the location of the stores that we use. For most of us, we don't need to look at fascias or windows to find the store; we just go through the operational task of getting to the doorway and entering. Our brain processes are focused on this mundane task and ignore any other information. When we are shopping in malls or streets that we are unfamiliar with, the fascia is practically invisible above our heads at an oblique angle. The bus stop signs sticking out perpendicular to the fascia are visible and we use the architecture that we are familiar with as well as the style of the window display, the typical design of the POS in the window, to recognize the store – but still, the view through the door is vital. The fact that we largely ignore any information outside a store is particularly evident with those shops that we use very frequently, (for example, the local corner store). We worked closely with a chain of convenience stores, and discovered that more than half of the people who were inside the store were unable to recall the name of the store that they were in. For them it was simply "the shop". Or else they remembered the name of the store that it used to be years ago.

Alongside this familiarity, expectation and routine, another issue is also at play when we ignore shop displays and point-of-sale advertising. When we conducted research with shoppers at petrol stations we discovered that the process of entering the store was so disruptive that by the time the person was inside they had forgotten anything they might have seen. Surely when a driver begins to fill their tank with petrol this is a great opportunity to communicate? Once you insert the pump and start filling the car you are effectively locked in position for a few minutes. We could see that most people seemed to look around them while they were attached to the pump, so it appeared that this would be a great opportunity to deliver marketing messages. We therefore measured the advertising on top of the pumps (where most people look as the rapidly escalating cost is displayed there), as well as adverts on the pump handle and on the shop window, all areas that shoppers seemed to be looking at. None of this advertising worked. We found that those who did notice something had forgotten it once they had gone through the door. In addition, when we are forced to do something like queue or stand involuntarily next to a pump, we tend to switch our attention away from the painful wait and think about other things, (for example, what we will do when we get to the end of the journey). The message has obviously not sunk in.

This point was clearly illustrated many times, notably when we interviewed a shopper who had stared at a display while waiting in a queue at a supermarket. What had she been thinking? Had any aspects of the display that she was looking at influenced any purchasing decisions? The answer: not at all. All that looking but no seeing; she was, in fact, thinking about what was on television that night.

You might be forgiven for asking: armed with this knowledge, what have most retailers done about their windows? The sad truth is … nothing. It is too challenging, it threatens accepted norms and so, amazingly, nothing is done. The industry continues to spend its potential profits on windows that don't generate sales and point of sale that has no influence on what shoppers do once they are inside the store.

So, what happens when we enter a store?

In our Dorothy Perkins research we discovered that shoppers do a "reconnaissance scan". This involves taking a quick look around the space, gauging its size and using the location of certain easy-to-identify products to build a mind map of the locations of different categories. This enables us to create a mental path that we proceed to follow around the store. Our brains are also processing other pieces of new information, including the smell, temperature, colours and lighting. Because we have finite attentional capacity, we tend to ignore everything outside of that reconnaissance scan. Consequently, our visual focus during this critical assimilation stage is on products that are within five to seven metres. Shoppers do not read signs.

Most of us can recall walking into a convenience store and beginning to shop but, as our hands fill up with items to buy, exclaiming "where's the basket!" (Or, at least, some of us – others go straight to the till.) This occurs despite having passed the baskets that are usually located by the door, but that went unnoticed when we walked in, because we were preoccupied with the reconnaissance scan. The "landing zone" at the entrance of the store often becomes an area of sensory overload: our visual attention is focused into the near distance and most of our unconscious processing is occupied with assessing and understanding the new environment that we have entered. One of our retail clients, taking notice of this, moved the basket stack from the front door to the end of the first and second aisles where shoppers could see them. Sales in the store increased by a remarkable 11 per cent – simply by moving the baskets.

A final, additional perspective on the challenges of arriving and entering stores is provided by perfume retailing. Most department stores around the world have their cosmetics and fragrance counters on the ground floor. As you walk in you are assailed by the smells and sights of beautiful staff, bright lights, glittering counters and an atmosphere heavy with perfume. Most department stores will rent the space to different fragrance houses, with the counter space closest to the entrance doors being the most expensive.

We studied how shoppers behaved with Lancôme, who had a perfume counter close to the door in London's Selfridges. Strangely, those people that shopped the counter appeared to be shopping the back, not the front of the counter. The whole point of the front counter design was to present its strongest display and communication to the shopper coming in. What we actually saw was that with this theatrical overload on the senses, the landing zone in this store was huge. Instead of the usual few paces, shoppers were several metres into the store before they started to really notice what was around them. This meant that they had already passed our counter.

In fact, Lancôme only attracted shoppers who were on their way out of the store, opposite to how the counter was designed. Worse still, they had potentially lost a sale to another perfume house deeper in the store, yet they were paying more for the privilege!

Once we're inside the store the issue of how we gravitate around is, of course, vitally important for retailers and brands. While this fact is appreciated by most forward-thinking businesses their responses are interestingly – and surprisingly – diverse. The next chapter explains this issue and describes some of the most significant factors at play when shoppers typically find their way around a chosen store.

4

A Voyage of Discovery

"I may not have gone where I intended to go but
I think I've ended up where I needed to be."
Douglas Adams

Close to where I live, a farmer has created a tourist attraction from six of his fields. Each year, he plants maize and when it's grown to about two metres tall he cuts pathways though it, creating a maize maze. Visitors delight in getting lost, a few successfully find their way around the maze to get out, and most of us need help to negotiate an exit. If asked to remember the layout of the maze simply by walking around it, could you? Is your memory up to the task?

Picture the grocery store where you do most of your shopping. In your mind, walk in through the front door; now, picture where the milk section is. Where is the bread aisle? The soft drinks aisle? Wine? Yoghurts? Washing and laundry products? Assuming that you do the shopping for your household fairly regularly, you will have been able to pinpoint where in the store to find these categories. It's not that you are particularly strange in being able to memorize the layout of a supermarket while being unable to recall the maze; it's actually a reflection of how our brains work and what we are designed to do.

The layout of a grocery store is also subject to the fickle interpretation of the human mind. When people write a shopping list, they will sometimes picture walking around the store. During this exercise, attention is paid to getting the items on the list in sequence with the layout in the store, to make the task of shopping more efficient. There is a motivation for doing this because if the sequence is correct, one is much less likely to miss anything on the list.

Even for the majority of us who prefer not to prepare shopping lists, forgetfulness is still unusual. Somehow, we are successful in restocking over 60 items when buying a big weekly shop for a family. It is pretty rare that we forget to buy what we need. This is another illustration of the power of the unconscious mind and how important it is when we go shopping.

When we recall the layout of, for example, a 60,000-square-foot store (equivalent in size to the farmer's maize fields) we are engaging in what is called *cognitive mapping*. The brain memorizes patterns of spaces and the routes to navigate them. For example, if you have a regular journey – say, driving home from work – you learn a cognitive map of the route. This means that you do not need to consider each turn at every junction or crossing and can instead function on an instinctive autopilot. This compares to an unfamiliar route, say to a friend's house in a town that you have never visited before, where you have to make directional and routing choices all the time. It is this use of the unconscious mind that results in most car accidents taking place in close proximity to the home: when the route is familiar, we pay drastically less attention to the journey. As you don't need to allocate attention to direction finding, you can lose sight of much of the environment around you.

It is cognitive mapping and our ability to operate on autopilot that leads to one of the most cited frustrations in food shopping: "When they move the store around".

This is frustrating because when we do the chore of the weekly shopping (and when we queue) we want to minimize the amount of conscious attention that we allocate to the task. Retailers used to think that it was a good idea to move categories around regularly, as it forced customers to pay attention and consider each purchase carefully. In fact, the opposite happens. If you corrupt the cognitive map, customers find it irritating and disruptive. It takes at least six months to fully learn the layout of a large supermarket. The brain's ability to process information is finite: if more attention is paid to navigating (thinking "what do I need, and where have they put it now?"), there is less capacity available to contemplate extra purchases.

Most of us go shopping without a list; we use the store itself as the shopping list to remind us of the things we have to buy. A memorized map of the route around the store acts as a mental cue to remind us what we need. If the layout changes those cues are lost. When they are working within a new layout, shoppers try to follow the same sequence of categories from the previous layout to make sure they don't forget to buy things. For example, the shopper can picture that milk came after yoghurts, and is now consciously looking for milk and ignoring anything that is not milk in order to find it. This way we walk past the display that the retailer wanted us to see, ignoring it completely.

This leads us to another retail myth. You may have wondered why it is that bread and milk, staple categories that you need to buy very frequently on shopping missions both large and small, are placed at the back of the supermarket. The myth goes that you will see a wide range of categories on the way to getting these staples and, along the way, decide to buy from them on impulse.

To understand why this is a myth let's imagine that you are a business person in the UK driving to visit a customer; it is lunchtime and you are hungry. In the UK, there is a strong lunchtime sandwich culture, and petrol stations usually stock the lunchtime staples – sandwiches, crisps and soft drinks. In a similar way to our other research, we have installed cameras in petrol stations to study the flows of customers. The dominant flow is the expected route from pump to door and on to the till, to pay for the fuel. There are many impulse opportunities here in what is known as the Grab Zone, the area where it is easiest to pick up additional items (such as confectionery) while in the queue.

The second most important flow is the sandwich/soft drink journey. The retailer we were studying had located these at the furthest distance from the door, with the other shelves angled so that on the route to the food and drink category you would see a wide range of other categories from which you could, ideally, make an impulse purchase. In reality, however, our hungry customers have one thing in mind, one task – lunch and the sandwiches. They go straight from the door to the sandwiches, without stopping on the way. Shoppers are in such a hurry to buy the items they intended on, that they pay absolutely no attention to the items they pass on the way – the complete reverse of the established myth. In truth, the shopper is only open to considering other categories once the planned task is completed. For this retailer, because the sandwiches and soft drinks were located at the back of the store, the shoppers had passed all the impulse categories during their cruise missile attack on the sandwiches – and so the retailer lost any extra sales opportunities.

We have countless records of shopper journeys in supermarkets on small top-up missions around the world, where shoppers come in with bread and milk-style staple categories in mind. The retailer has fallen for the myth and put them at the back of the store and the shopper trails for miles around the store, ignoring everything until the task categories are collected. Of course, by this time the shopper is two-thirds of the way around the store and now looking for the shortest route back to the tills, missing all those impulse opportunities. Instead, if the retailer manages the shopper's time efficiently and respectfully, the customer is much more likely to return for future shopping missions. A better store layout encourages loyalty. Part of the reason behind the success of Waitrose's ground-breaking, multi-mission store was that by analyzing shoppers' cognitive maps they could engineer the store layout to better resonate with them. Customers may spend less time in the store, but they spend more per trip and they visit the store more frequently. Efficient layout is one of the drivers of customer loyalty.

The cognitive map is the reason why so many supermarkets and hypermarkets are badly laid out. It is another example of the difference between our perceptions of how we shop and the reality of how we actually shop. If you go to a large supermarket in a developed market, say France, and interview shoppers about how they shopped in the store, around 25 per cent of the shoppers would tell the interviewer that they shopped throughout the whole store (that is, they went up and down every aisle in the store). Retailers around the world have done this research, and believing that lots of shoppers snake up and down every aisle, the store is laid out in a logical progression of adjacent categories. Well, we have already seen that the majority of shoppers are really doing small basket shops, so that type of layout is not going to work for them. But, the retailer reasons, at least the main shopper sounds like they are working their way logically around the store, and because they are the ones that spend the most money, the layout works.

So we took the 25 per cent of shoppers that had told the interviewer they had browsed the whole store and looked at the film of them shopping. Fewer than two per cent of them covered more than half of the store. It was clear that the massive discrepancy between perception and reality was caused by cognitive mapping. These shoppers had learnt the cognitive map of the store for a large, main shopping expedition. They will have followed their map around the store. In reality though, if you don't have a cat or a dog, you won't visit the pet food aisle, if you don't have a baby you'll miss that aisle, and many items like laundry and oral care can be to are visited far less frequently. Suddenly, what is perceived as a big weekly shop in fact only covers a relatively small proportion of the total store space. Significantly, because of these category miss outs, the "logical" layout of categories becomes nonsensical.

In fact, in large supermarkets, the average shopping trip will cover less than one-third of the store, and in the typical mass merchandisers in North America, shoppers will only cover about 20 per cent of the store. It's worth remembering the point we made in Chapter One: stores like supermarkets are not selling spaces; they are warehouses where people collect products in much the same way that a warehouse worker will pick goods from an order form. The warehouse worker is not going to go up and down every single aisle; it would be crazily inefficient.

I was always puzzled about why shoppers would tell interviewers that their shop had a good layout, when by looking at the plan of the store I could see that the layout was completely impractical. These shoppers had simply learnt the layout and they were matching their mission-based cognitive maps to the space. Once they had done that, the shopper was going to be satisfied and it almost didn't matter how badly the store was laid out. You will find that these retailers have lower spending per customer as the shoppers' time is used less efficiently.

In markets where modern trade stores are less familiar, for example in South-East Asia, huge hypermarkets are also used in another, different way. As well as the functional main and top-up shopping missions, we also see the store being used as a leisure shop. Whereas a typical 100,000-square-foot store in the US will be shopped on average in about 25 minutes, the same size store with a similar layout and broadly similar product categories is shopped in about 50 minutes in Asia. Around ten per cent of shoppers will spend over an hour shopping the store as a treat for themselves, buying from three or four categories, and they might do this a couple of times a month, particularly at weekends. Unlike in European and North American stores, shoppers in Asia can be seen devoting a far greater amount of time to their shopping – for example, picking up and reading packaging, almost regardless of the category.

My colleague, Herb Sorensen, developed another way of studying store usage, one that avoided having to use cameras to study the behaviour of shoppers. With the agreement of the store and its customers, we fixed Radio Frequency Identification (RFID) tags to the trolleys in the store. Each RFID tag broadcasts a unique signal to readers built into the ceiling of the store, enabling us to study hundreds of thousands of trips around the store. We were able to monitor each trolley and evaluate each shopper's journey to identify where they stopped and use the sales data from the store about to to evaluate what was purchased (completely anonymously, as far as the shopper was concerned).

Taking on this innovation, one of my colleagues, Susan Thomas, has put permanent installations into several stores around the world that give years of reporting. The data from this research is fascinating. In a typical, large north European supermarket, the average time spent in the store is 28.5 minutes. This has declined by seven minutes over the past ten years, as shoppers carry out more, smaller shopping trips. Nearly half of this time is spent in transit, travelling from one category to the next. The average journey around the store is 0.5km long. It takes about 28 minutes to conduct the small basket shop (less than £15 spent) and 35 minutes for the average large shop (over £50). The average large shopping trip only travels 95m further than the smallest basket trip! These data highlight how poorly normal supermarkets cater for their largest volume of visitors.

So, how easy is it to learn the layout to your 60,000-square-foot supermarket – is it just a matter of visiting the maze the same number of times? The answer is no. It is not just the directional choices we make that create the cognitive map; it is the accompanying visual cues as well. One element that makes the supermarket easier to learn is identifying what the different categories look like. In any store, whether it's a supermarket, fashion outlet or DIY retailer, we use products to recognize different categories.

We were asked by Focus DIY to investigate their store layout that was modelled using the "racetrack" principle. Here, the shopper enters the store and joins a wide rectangular walkway that mimics the shape of the store, but instead of running around the walls' edges, there are categories on both sides as you walk around. The idea is to manage the shoppers' journey so that they pass all the categories, again to facilitate potential impulse purchasing. The idea is that they may want, say, a lamp in addition to the paint that they had come in to buy. But this doesn't take account of the missions that form the main reasons for the store visit in the first place – and the DIY store visitor is almost invariably. on a project-focused visit. Shoppers entering the store looking for paint ignore the wide, carefully-constructed walkways that ferry them on a detour around the store. Instead, and not too surprisingly, they look for paint. Once they see the visual cue of shelves of paint cans shoppers simply choose the most direct route to that category.

So we found that for Focus, their racetrack was not used as intended, but there were a series of cut-through routes to the main destination categories. The layout, which had been carefully planned to pass the shopper by logical category adjacencies, say wallpaper, then paste, then brushes, wasn't working. The paint shopper went straight across the racetrack, through screws and fixings, across one of the lighting aisles and into the paint aisle. Just as you see the well-worn track of dead grass across the park from one gate to the other and a deserted, paved path that meanders around the edge via a scenic pond and lovely views, so it is that we take what we assess to be the most direct route to get to our destination. Again, shoppers obey the law of entropy. When shopping, we are much more likely (and prefer) to use the products themselves to find our way, rather than rely on signs. It irritates us when we are in the type of DIY store that has tall, cavernous aisles that limit visibility to a single aisle, forcing us to wander down endless corridors looking for a written sign.

How does it work when we are looking for these products? Particularly in grocery stores, where categories can look similar (for example, canned products), how do we differentiate between different sections and categories?

The answer lies in the use of *signpost brands* – brands that are so recognizable that they describe the category. We use them to unconsciously alert us to the boundaries between the different categories that we are navigating. For example, Coca-Cola signals the presence of soft drinks, Evian and Perrier signal bottled water, and so on. These signposts are the most iconic representations of the category, but not always the best sellers. Coca-Cola is often not the market leader in countries where private labels are strong, but shoppers still use it as a marker to navigate the aisles. We tend to walk along the main transit aisles, either the cross break (the big aisle that runs down the centre of the store), the top break (the aisle that runs along the back of the store), or the racetrack (for example, in US mass merchandisers like Walmart). We glance down the aisles, usually towards the central bays, and use the signpost brands to identify what is there and whether we need to visit.

Even if they don't intend to buy the brand, a shopper is most likely to look at the signpost brand first. Also, in large categories such as spirits, there will be secondary signpost brands for different subcategories (for example, gin, vodka, whisky). In turn, this determines the search pattern that the shopper uses to find the item they want to buy. However, not every category has a signpost brand. Because of the nature of the display, frozen food doesn't really have a brand that signposts it, as the products are hidden in wells and behind doors; the banks of freezers, themselves, signal the category. Wine is similar: there are no established brands that are iconic for the category so the rows of green and brown bottles signpost the category.

Highlighting the signpost brand can help the category's visibility and its sales. We studied the beer category for Guinness. We filmed shoppers and discovered that most shoppers came into the aisle and bought either lager or bitter, then u-turned and moved back out of the aisle, much of the time not even reaching the stout category where Guinness was located. We also eye-tracked shoppers in this category to find out how they recognized it and what elements helped them find it.

It was clear that Guinness was the signpost for its category – but, aside from the colour black, there is no major feature of the Guinness packaging for shoppers to identify. From Guinness' marketing team, we discovered that people identified them with the poured-out product in a Guinness glass. Consequently, we designed a simple fixture with a four-foot tall cutout of the Guinness glass printed in black with a white head. After placing one of these on either side of the stout category, we filmed its effect on shoppers. Immediately, sales for stout increased by 23 per cent and sales for beer overall went up by four per cent. The fixture was not diverting shoppers to substitute another brand for Guinness. Instead, the icon was drawing in more shoppers from the main beer aisle to buy more of all the competing products.

Having used the eye-tracker to establish both the existence and the role of signpost brands in category recognition and store navigation, we thought it would be important to explore what happened in the brain in response to visual cues. We set up a project with Professor Gemma Calvert of Warwick University in the UK and owner of Neurosense – a company that specializes in using the various technologies of neuroscience. We recruited shoppers and asked them to come to the lab at Kings College, London, where we had specially-adapted fMRI (Functional Magnetic Resonance Imaging) scanners to take eye-tracking scans. fMRI involves putting the respondent on a bed that is introduced into a large, doughnut-shaped ring. Inside this ring is a magnet that allows the scientist to see where extraordinary activity occurs in the brain, compared with the normal activity that happens all the time. This is measured by a scan conducted every couple of seconds that highlights the blood flow and identifies the active parts of the brain.

We pre-recorded a film of the shoppers' field of view as they approached and entered the aisle for two categories, coffee and detergent. Having settled onto the bed, the respondents inside the fMRI machines watched this film as though they were travelling down the aisles, allowing us to combine eye-tracking with a map of neurological activity triggered by the shop layout. For the first time ever, we combined an eye-track of the elements of the scene that the shopper had looked at with the resultant brain activity.

The results were both fascinating and unexpected. First, we saw that signpost brands did more than just identify a category: they activated the brain's reward centre. Certain brands have the power to inspire positive memories in the brain while others repulse potential buyers. Seeing the signpost brand, the shopper's brain showed anticipation of reward, typical of when we are about to buy something we like. The brain also altered the way it processed visual attention, from simply reviewing the scene to allocating attention to a search. It also appeared that a "script" of learnt behaviour was being activated by signpost brands. We learnt that not only did the signpost help the shopper to navigate and find the category, it seemed to prepare the shopper for the process of shopping that category.

Whether or not we have a list, we walk around the store using the signpost brands located on our cognitive maps to trigger small learnt behavioural scripts, particularly in the categories where we regularly shop. We have literally learnt to shop in the same way that someone doing a repetitive task on a factory production line repeats the same action time after time. Every time we come to, say, the milk category, we perform the same visual and physical actions to buy the product that we normally buy.

Having discovered the power of signposts it's worth considering: what does the typical path of a grocery shopper look like in a large supermarket? For the main weekly shopper, the journey begins when we enter the store, usually having collected the trolley first. Quite a few shoppers will dawdle at the entrance, almost putting off the start of the task by browsing the flowers or newsstand. Then we head into the fresh produce section and start the first phase of shopping: meal building. For most of us this entails buying a repeated stock of items that we always buy for possibly two or three main meals over the next few days. After a fairly uncontrolled flow around fresh produce, we usually head to the top part of the store and start to use the top or cross break to move through the store. Quite often there is some organized snaking up and down of the first few aisles. After this, we change to the stocking up phase, again working either with a list or more likely, using the store like a larder, perusing the signpost brands of categories to mentally take stock of what we need. Here, any logical flow from one aisle to the next generally stops and shoppers run up one side of an aisle, skip one or two aisles and then return down the next aisle.

Once we reach the end of the store, we then flow down into the bottom half of the store, returning back towards the door. Again we travel down one aisle, skip a few of them and then return. But now we are much more likely to stop shopping and move towards the checkouts. Only a few shoppers will return all the way back to the front part of the store before paying for their weekly shopping. For most of them, and for the top-up shoppers as well, the general merchandise area (including clothing, homewares and CDs) that is generally at the front of the store is not heavily used – although stores that have health and beauty categories first do draw shoppers into that area before proceeding to the main food area.

The top-up shopper uses the space differently. Having collected a carrier, the top-up shopper usually moves into the fresh produce section where he takes a single route before coming to the cross break and moves quickly along this transit route, dipping into aisles, u-turning back out onto the transit route and quite often switching up to the top break to reach the far part of the store. Next, he returns back through the store through two or three access aisles down to the checkouts. Top-up shoppers usually arrive with a small number of pre-planned categories: fresh produce, dairy and bread. They are more likely to purchase on impulse or to switch from their planned selection, and their expenditure per minute in the store is far higher than for any other shopping mission.

Shoppers tire as they go through the store. As we saw earlier, the average shopper covers half a kilometre. Wanting to finish the trip, shoppers shop faster and faster as they get further through the shop. Other measures (such as blink rate) slow, and we generally process less and less information, as all the intense visual data that confronts us starts to overload the brain. In an investigation into shoppers' purchases of salad dressing in US retailers, we found that when the category was located in a part of the store that was visited early, such as in the fresh produce section, customers spent an average of 28 seconds there. When the same category with the same display was located at the far end of the shop, shoppers only spent 8.5 seconds there.

The convenience channel is growing rapidly around the world. The reasons for this vary: in emerging markets, they form a direct replacement for traditional "mom and pop" stores. In developed markets they are popular because they are easier for small, quick basket shopping, with people often using large supermarkets for big shopping trips and using the convenience store every couple of days to top up. In several countries, notably the US, pharmacies are extending their product range to include grocery items, adding additional convenience.

Typically there are ranges of goods in convenience stores that satisfy an immediate need (soft drinks, snack foods) and smaller selections of replacement items than you would see in a supermarket (ie, soups, fresh produce). There is a wide range of missions going on in these convenience stores – for example: lunchtime and snacking, meal for tonight, emergency run-outs as well as small top-ups. For that reason, shoppers' use of these spaces is driven towards time efficiency and getting in and out of the store as quickly as possible. However, despite a planned style of shopping and a focus on a particular mission, many shoppers will buy products from categories they hadn't intended to before arriving at the store. This is often the home of impulse purchasing.

Again, shoppers regularly use the same stores for the same purpose. Usually, more than two-thirds of the people in a store will visit it at least every two or three days and will have mission-based cognitive maps of the store in their minds. Even more than in the large supermarkets, shoppers are operating in a way that is mainly unconscious, using signpost brands as visual cues and applying learnt scripts of behaviour. We are more likely to see men in these convenience stores but the majority is still female.

A major feature of these stores is how their use varies throughout the day. This can be so pronounced that convenience stores in Japan actually move categories around to reflect this. At the beginning of the day shoppers come to buy newspapers, from mid-morning onwards shoppers visit to buy pre-packed lunches (such as sushi), and into the evening it is magazines and chilled wines that become popular. As a result of these predictable, shifting patterns of behaviour the fixtures with these products are moved to the front of the store. In fact, you are very likely to see several vending machines outside selling tobacco, soft drinks and sushi so the shopper doesn't even have to enter the store.

An important point is that we don't spend long shopping times in these stores, usually around five minutes, and up to half of that time is spent on the actual transaction of queuing and waiting to pay. We either travel around the perimeter of the store or we just walk straight towards the counter, possibly dipping into an aisle on the way. The "perfect store" project that we conducted for Unilever and Co-op was valuable because it helped us understand the category sequences that the differing missions required and it focused our thinking on how to make sure that the layout supported a range of different missions. The model has been adapted by Unilever to help with the layout of convenience stores, benefiting retailers and customers around the world.

In countries where traditional "mom and pop" stores still dominate, they are used differently. These stores are shopped even more frequently, sometimes several times a day. The role of the storekeeper is often pivotal. In India, the shopper, usually a man, gives the list to the storekeeper who then proceeds to select the products, often making key choices on behalf of the shopper. These stores are often cluttered and the many pieces of point-of-sale material provided by the manufacturers only add to it, rather than simplifying the process.

These stores often have customers who have shopped there for generations and often offer credit facilities to their shoppers. This makes for an intense, societal relationship between shopper and retailer. The retailer's role is deeply rooted in the customers' lives and the retailer often lives in the store, connecting him even further to the community. For example, in Honduras, a large minority of residential "mom and pop" stores refuse to stock alcohol in deference to their customers' religious and societal beliefs.

In other countries, a large number of retailers don't have a physical store; they are mobile, either bringing their goods out onto the street in carts, or daily setting up their display in a street market. Where there is also a modern trade presence, they may well buy their stock from those retailers as they can be cheaper than the wholesaler. Some street traders will break up the packaging and target the lowest income shopper by selling individual cigarettes or smaller pouches of washing powder that they have made.

Whilst these retailers are not so concerned about how their shoppers navigate around the store, they will often be very experienced in knowing how the flow of potential shoppers approach their pitch, and therefore they often think about merchandising and display in relation to this.

Because of this research and experience, we now understand the different ways that stores are used – and why. What matters are not simply the categories that are in a store but also the signposts that illustrate where those categories are and the reason we are there – the mission that we are on. There are also architectural biases affecting how shoppers move around, particularly in retail sectors that are not heavily planned or frequently visited, such as department stores. Again, without being consciously aware, we read architectural signals and they influence how we move around those spaces. We first noticed this when we were asked to work with the UK retailer Marks and Spencer (M&S). My colleague, Andrew Freer, and I were in the store to review the layout and in particular, circulation routes. On paper, it all seemed to make sense: there was a hard surface walkway from the door that, as usual, joined a race track walkway around the store.

Andrew and I stood in the store for several hours watching the shoppers, and we were struck by how few were on the racetrack. Our expectation, with our background in retail design, was that this should be the busiest place for most shoppers. In reality, people seemed to be buried in the sea of merchandise that ran up to the walkway, and not just because they were shopping there. We moved over to the area containing the most people moving around so we could investigate. Shoppers appeared to be navigating across men's trousers and following a line between the fixtures. We were between men's shirts and men's shoes and this line had not been planned by the store as an access route at all. We went to some of the other areas where shoppers appeared to be gathered, again moving around but not shopping. They seemed to be moving parallel to the racetrack, but some ten metres within the department. As usual, the racetrack followed the line of the exterior walls but was situated to allow one department's depth between the wall and the walkway. Finally after some time, we realized what was happening. The ceiling nearest to the walls was lowered into the store for a lighting effect. Shoppers were unconsciously following the line of this lowered ceiling!

We saw the same effect some years later during a project for Debenhams, a UK department store. We installed cameras in the store and were following the movements around the homewares floor. This was fed by an escalator that landed shoppers directly onto a hard floor racetrack walkway. All of the departments, bedding, kitchenware, etc, were carpeted. Unlike our DIY and M&S examples, the shoppers were delivered onto the racetrack – and it appeared they were stuck on it. When we analyzed the results of the filming, we saw that nearly all of the shoppers stayed on the racetrack and seemed only to interact with fixtures that were adjacent to it. Hardly anyone ventured off the racetrack and into the product areas of the store. Because there was a sensory change when crossing the line from hard to soft flooring and the strong visual line that divided the hard floor from the carpet, shoppers unconsciously did not cross the line. Instead, we had film of shoppers stretching to reach products from the walkway while making sure their feet stayed on the walkway!

We see that in task or mission-based stores, shoppers use their cognitive maps and signposts to make their way around. This is different from stores where there is much less task-based shopping and much more browsing. Here, in addition to the visual cue of the product as a signpost, we also rely more on the unconscious signals of flooring and fixture layouts to guide our movement around the store. There is one other interesting area of retailing that is still growing fast that we haven't yet discussed: shopping online.

The UK has the world's highest proportion of regular online food shoppers and the numbers are continuing to grow. This online success is the result of a combination of a few major food retailers, dense urban populations in close proximity (that allow easier home delivery) and a particularly British focus on time. It is certainly not the design of the websites. It is apparent that website designers have no concept of how shoppers shop, how they move from one category to the next using signpost brands or how they like to build meals and then top up the cupboards, etc. The sites are little more than large databases and access to them is slow and difficult. All the cues that shoppers have learnt over years of shopping in stores are gone. This is why so many of the people that visit the sites for the first time simply give up, while over 80 per cent of people that do use them rely on their "favourites" list and avoid the difficulty of having to wade through the database. A memorable example of this occurred in the early years of online shopping, when we were researching one of the sites for Walkers Crisps. Without a doubt, Walkers is the signpost brand for crisps in stores. And while the site we tested did at least have photos of the pack to help shoppers find their products, we found that Walkers, because of starting with the letter "W", was buried away on page two, because that was how the crisps category was organized.

We have been working with virtual stores since their origins in the mid-1990s. Our first project in this area was with Salford University and the Co-op, one of the first retailers in the world to build a fully-interactive virtual store. Salford built a fully-immersive environment, with shoppers putting on a pair of goggles with a computer image projected onto each lens that created a sense of 3D space. These shoppers were able to move around the store using a computerized trolley handle, while a specially-fitted glove monitored the movement of the shopper's hand – enabling the user to control their actions in the virtual shop as they would in reality. The shopper could reach out and pick up a full 3D product and place it in their trolley. It was truly amazing to move around this virtual space. The more time that you spent in the store, the more your brain was tricked into believing that you were really there.

We were keen to see how shoppers would behave in this environment. In particular, would people start to act differently once they were wearing large goggles, grasping a pretend trolley handle with no trolley attached and wearing a strange glove with wires running out of it? We made sure we recruited typical shoppers, including older shoppers with little or no experience at all of computers and computing. The key question was this: after a short training period, would a woman my grandmother's age who harboured the greatest suspicion of an ATM be able to adapt and operate in this bizarrely-real environment using state of the art computing equipment?

The answer, amazingly, was yes. We found that around 90 per cent of the key behaviours that you would expect to see in the real world were played out in this virtual world. Because the virtual store had been modelled on the store that these shoppers regularly used, all the familiar cues were there. We watched as be-goggled shoppers pushed and steered their floating handles and waved their gloves around, completely understanding and believing in this new virtual world.

Today, virtual reality is used quite heavily to measure shopper behaviour without ever having to visit a store. The quality of the graphics compared to those of the Co-op stores is immeasurably improved, and there is no longer any need to wear goggles and gloves. We also regularly use eye tracking in this virtual world. Total superstores such as Tesco in the UK and mass merchandisers like Walmart in the US have been built not only with all the correct products but with realistic shelves. The metal gleams as it would in-store, and the floors are tiled the same way as in a real store, etc. Shoppers move around the store, pick up products from the shelves, read packaging and select their products. Across North America there are now well over 50 locations where consumers are recruited to shop these virtual stores and test new layouts, ideas for displays, new ways of arranging products and new packaging. We have run trials where we filmed shoppers in a specific store, modelled that store in virtual reality and then asked shoppers to shop in that virtual store. Replicated behaviour – meaning that what happens in the store also happens in the virtual world – is over 95 per cent present.

In the early days of virtual stores, the amount of computer memory processing required was huge. Displays would take days of processing by massive machines in order to render a single image. Today these stores are tested running off a laptop. Broadband width will soon mean that we can start to use these stores to replace the database experience of online stores. As these new, online virtual stores learn the routes that you take and the categories you typically visit, they will remodel themselves to make your journey more efficient for you. Each one of us will have our own virtual store laid out to suit the particular way that we want to shop. Our individual nature of shopping is also explored in the next chapter, where we explain how the way that our eyes and minds work affects our attention and how this in turn, affects a range of other issues including advertising, packaging and marketing.

5

What Do We See?

*"Every person takes the limits of their own field
of vision for the limits of the world."*
Arthur Schopenhauer

The 12th century village of Hallaton in the English Midlands was a natural meeting place. At the junction of five roads that followed a line of gently undulating hills and valleys, Hallaton was a meeting place for many travellers. This was especially the case at Easter, when the village played neighbouring Medbourne at Bottle Kicking, a sport like rugby but without rules. With the travellers came news from near and far, shared in the four pubs in the village in the form of tales and sometimes song.

Often those tales and stories were cyclical (from which we get the verse, chorus, verse, chorus form of popular song) and they relied on established images to communicate ideas. From the time of our earliest ancestors until the 17th century, our primary means of communication was oral. The invention of printing technology effected a radical change in society, not only in the means of communication that was increasingly visual, but also in how people communicated. Writing allowed a linear, complex story to be told unlike in the cyclic, oral tradition.

In his book, *Orality and Literacy*, Walter J. Ong discusses how it is that writing distances the originator of a thought from the recipient. In addition, the further entrenched that writing becomes as a mode of expression, the more it is that humans move from an oral and aural-based sensory world to one where vision reigns supreme. The 20th century accelerated this move towards a visually-dominant world with the landmark invention and widespread popularity of television and computing.

Our eyes dominate what we do and how we behave. Set a task and an environment in which to do it and our eyes will explore that environment and inform us how we can complete the task. Shopping is no different. We set ourselves a task – for example, one of the missions that we discussed earlier – and we choose an environment to suit that mission.

This chapter is about understanding what we see when we go shopping. So much of what retailers and brands do is designed to target and harness the power of visual influences: from advertising through store design to packaging. Given that fact and the power of the visual, it is perhaps surprising how little these industries know and understand about how our eyes work and how we process visual information. Interestingly, our relatively recent switch from oral to predominantly visual does not mean that this primary method of communication is more successful. The volume of visual information that we are expected to process and act on has increased dramatically over the past 100 years. For example, if you look at black and white photographs of a typical High Street in the early 20th century, some of the stores have a name over the doorway and the street scene itself is notable for the dominance of pedestrians. Review that same street today and you will see that in addition to an increase in the number of people there will also be cars, buses, outdoor advertising, glitzy fascias and bright windows, etc. Our world today is dramatically different from that of the recent past in many ways, but among the most notable of these differences is the volume and intensity of marketing activity that tries to blast though our visual senses and gain our attention.

Reflecting on the relative lack of understanding about how our eyes work and how we process visual information when shopping, we decided to investigate how many brand messages we receive in a single day. To do this, we recruited some people to wear baseball caps that had been adapted to carry tiny video cameras that would record what they could see. We then watched the video and counted how many times these people had been exposed to messaging, whether through primary marketing media such as television, or secondary mechanics like a store's branded carrier bag. The participants all lived in urban environments in the UK and put the cap on when they dressed in the morning and, barring moments of necessary privacy, only removed the cap when they went to bed at night. The average number of brand exposures for our respondents was 3,000 messages per day. We also asked people how many brand messages they could remember from these 3,000, and the average recall was ... one. Now there are a couple of caveats to these data. First, just because the respondent had an opportunity to see this advertising since it was in front of them did not mean that they had either looked at or seen it (even though this is a key measure for advertising). Second, a lack of conscious recall does not necessarily mean that a message was not processed and stored by the brain. Even so, this remarkable discrepancy between 3,000 messages and one recall begs the question: why is this?

It is a common misconception that we "see" everything that is in front of us, because this is how it feels. Just because we have a field of view of about 200 degrees certainly does not mean that we are processing and using that total field of view. A popular experiment to illustrate this point was designed by Daniel Simons of the University of Illinois and Chris Chabris of Harvard University. They showed a short, 30-second film and asked volunteers to count the number of times a group of people dressed in white T-shirts threw a basketball to each other, and then asked them what else they had seen (at the same time there was a team dressed in black). In their test well over 50 per cent did not notice a woman in a gorilla suit walk through the scene, and those who were asked to give a more demanding account were even less likely to see the gorilla. I've used the film over 100 times all over the world with audiences of as many as 3,500 people and more typically, with groups of 20 – 100 people. I consistently find that about 20 per cent of people will see the gorilla, while the remainder are amazed to see her when they are shown the film again (the usual response is that I have switched the film). It seems incredible that in a relatively simple scene, most of us miss a two-metre gorilla beating its chest in the middle of the picture. This is called *inattentional blindness* and Chabris and Simons have written a book about this experiment and others that illustrate this feature of our visual processing.

The film with the gorilla works because of the way that we actually see. Of all the elements of any scene in front of you, you will take in only about one per cent and actually process about five per cent of that one per cent. So our vision processing system is designed to discard information, rather than to gather it. At any one time our brains are only capable of processing seven bits of visual information. In order to avoid massive overload, our eyes sample small parts of the scene and use (among other things) pattern recognition to fill in the rest.

It is worth exploring this process in a little more detail. The scene in front of us enters through the lens of the eye and is projected on the back of the eyeball onto the retina. The retina is made up of tiny cells called photoreceptors of which there are two main types: rods and cones. Rods are adapted for low light usage. For example, when we go outside from a brightly illuminated room into a dark night, it takes 5 – 10 minutes for our night vision to start working. This is because the brain is dialling up information from the rods and reducing that from the cones.

Cones are adapted for colour, intensity and depth perception and actually do most of our seeing. Cones are mainly concentrated onto a small central part of the retina known as the fovea, and this area is responsible for just about all of what we can see. Rather than the potential 200 degrees of the visual field, we are in fact channelling our sight through only one or two degrees. To get an idea of the size of this area, hold out your hand as though you were thumbing a lift. Look at your thumbnail: this is roughly the size of what is known as *foveal attention*. Around 50 per cent of the connections to the optic nerve come from this tiny area.

When we "see" a scene, we rapidly shift our gaze across it to bring different portions into foveal attention. When you watch eye movement using an eye-tracker, the equipment is designed to show where foveal attention rests in a scene. It does this by superimposing a cross-hair target onto the video of the field of view. The watcher sees the cross-hairs jump and stop momentarily, then jump again, then stop, jump, etc. These two eye movements are called *saccades* (the jumps) and *fixations* (the stops). The fixation lasts somewhere between 100 – 600 milliseconds and at that point information is being sent back to the brain. During the saccade, which lasts 20 – 200 milliseconds and is the fastest movement produced by the human body, no information is sent back so as to avoid sending a blurred image caused by the movement.

During the fixation, which is the moment when foveal attention rests or is fixed, in addition to processing information about the scene, the brain diverts covert attention to it and uses what is called a *saliency map*. This investigates features of the scene that are potentially worthy of attention and fixation. The next saccade-fixate is determined by the task or training (for example, looking for white T-shirts) or by an unusual shape, light, movement, etc. Given that our vision evolved when we were hunter-gatherers, movement or an unusual shape was fundamental to our survival: there could be a sabre-toothed tiger arriving on the scene while we were fixating on the task of picking berries.

Now let's return to the experiment with the gorilla video. When we eye-track people watching the gorilla film we often see that people fixate on the gorilla although they don't actually "notice" it. Why does this happen? Clearly, the fixation itself is not enough. That is because the way that we gather and process information normally depends on the task. When I brief people to watch the gorilla movie, I ask them to follow the team dressed in white as they pass the ball from one to another. This means that when we fixate on the gorilla (which is black), our task generally overrides the information or regards it as irrelevant, therefore we do not "see" it.

Given that we only process seven bits of information at any one time, our allocation of what we actually need to pay attention to is therefore very selective. Another great example of this is provided by Chabris and Simons in their book, *The Invisible Gorilla*. This was an adapted version of the gorilla experiment: an unexpected object was introduced while the respondents were talking on their mobile phones. In this situation, where attention was allocated to their phone calls, 90 per cent missed the element of the unexpected. Clearly, it is not the physical act of holding a phone in your hand that is the danger when you are driving. It is the allocation of attention away from driving to the telephone conversation that makes you dangerous.

We can also adapt our attention so that we are able to ignore strong sensory inputs. For example, when I was a child I visited my Aunt Ro and Uncle Michael with my parents. I remember arriving on a sunny day and sitting outside, which would have been nice were it not for the fact that they lived directly under the flight path into London's Heathrow airport, one of the busiest airports in the world. Every three minutes a massive jet came roaring overhead and conversation stopped as we took an aural battering. "How do you cope?" we all asked, not a little stunned. "Oh, you get used to it and don't notice it anymore" they replied.

We start connecting meanings with patterns from the very moment we are born. As our eyes slowly adjust to the bright light attending that moment, we start to learn that the pattern in front of us along with its smell and warmth, is "mother" and we soon learn that this pattern feeds us when we are hungry. It is estimated that it takes us around 15 minutes from the moment we are born to learn our mother's face. We grow from this stage and we continue to process a vast amount of information, making associations between visual stimuli and memories, and connecting these patterns with meanings and values. This forging of connections that describes the connections between neurons is the basis of memory.

When considering what it is that we see and how we process visual information, we need to be clear about what memory is. Traditional ways of researching memory encompassed asking people to memorize images or items and then test their recall. Most of our memory, however, is not "forced" recall like this. In these traditional tests, the subject memorizes certain information because the examiner has asked him to – so the decision to memorize rests with the examiner, not the subject. This doesn't replicate memory because memory recall is best understood as a means to an end, not the end itself.

Memory is created by billions of neurons that are the cells that make up our brains. Neurons, connected by gaps called synapses, communicate across these gaps with neurotransmitters. Once neurons have fired in sequence they are then sensitised to be more likely to fire in sequence again – this is the basis of memory. In response to a repeated stimulation for example, looking at something that you have seen before – the same sequence of neurons will fire. Baroness Susan Greenfield, Professor of Pharmacology at Oxford University and a renowned neuroscientist, calls these *neuronal clouds,* and these clouds have millions of connections to other memories.

Our memories are not located in one place in the brain, they are distributed and dormant. Take for example my memory of Heinz Tomato Ketchup. I have a visual memory of the brand; I also have a memory of the sensory experience of pouring it, a sense of its taste, a motor memory of the motion of opening the bottle and pouring the content, and partly because this has often been advertised I also have a memory of how long it used to take to come out of the bottle. I even have a visual and phonetic memory of the words. Sadly, I also have a memory of being in a restaurant, shaking the bottle, the top flying off and ketchup exploding all over me, my guests and the diners at nearby tables. My memory of this product is also associated with other things and people: fish fingers, chips, peas, plates, my godson pouring it over all his food, my son spreading it on his face, over kitchen surfaces, in cafes, etc.

It is my working memory operating from the front part of the brain, the frontal lobes, which organizes the memories required for whatever task is occupying me at a particular moment. My brain is continuously drawing in and discarding memories, depending on the task at hand. For example, if I am to use the tomato ketchup, my working memory calls up a memory of where it is in the kitchen, then a memory of how to hold it, how to open and how to pour it. I don't need to consciously call up these memories; the memories and their sequence are organized automatically.

A memory is also strengthened or weakened by emotion. The memory attached to ketchup is strong for me partly because of the feelings of embarrassment and humour that came from throwing it around in a restaurant. Memories, however, do not necessarily need to be surrounded by emotions for them to be strong or durable. For example, picture the chest of drawers that you had in your bedroom as a young adult. There are probably not many strong emotions related to this memory, yet because you saw it every day the memory "path"was repeatedly trodden and, as a result, is strong. You can probably remember the weight of the drawers as they opened, perhaps how you organized them (or didn't).

As you might expect, all of these factors have a dramatic effect on the success or failure of marketing. Yet despite its power, the marketing industry largely ignores this science. Most of a brand's concentration is on consumers (people that have bought something and are using it) rather than on shoppers (who are looking for something to buy), meaning that they focus on how good a product is to use. Yet clearly the gatekeeper to becoming a consumer is being a shopper. No matter how good a product is, until someone buys it the consumption experience remains inactivated.

The problem is that many people expect advertising to do too much. They not only want it to build meaning and value around a brand but, because they mistakenly think of a store as a place where selling happens, advertising also has to be some kind of silent salesman. As we said earlier, stores are warehouses: places we go to fulfil our mission and collect the items we want. The amount of time spent in a store choosing and deciding what brand to buy is negligible. Despite this, some advertisers seem to imagine that seeing the product in-store will somehow stimulate the advert to play in the shoppers' heads and remind them of why they should buy it.

Packaging often becomes the link to advertising for products as it is seen both by shoppers and consumers, and is highly influential on whether a product is purchased. Typically, when a product is being developed or launched, the packaging design is researched using focus groups. A new design is brought to the group and is discussed for an hour or so of the group session. This is probably the only time – and certainly the longest time – that people outside the producing company itself spend this long considering the product.

If eye-tracking technology is used to test how a package will appear on the shelf, it tends to be laboratory-based using static eye-tracking. This is when a test candidate sits on a chair and is asked to look at a projection of a shelf that includes the new design. In reality, however, the shopper will never view the product like this. Just as with the approach to the store front, the shopper almost always approaches the fixture at an oblique angle while moving. This means that the only data you will get from fixed eye-tracking studies is how someone would look at the product if they were sitting on a chair in their kitchen looking at the product on their shelf; it does not represent how the shopper would find it in the store.

All the discovery work that we do to research the potential performance of the product doesn't involve the one scenario that needs to happen to make the product a success: someone in a store actually shopping for that product. One of the things we learnt when we started using eye-tracking in stores was how few fixations shoppers used to recognize the products that they were buying, particularly those they bought regularly. When analysing the data from a total shop we found that over two-thirds of all the fixations during shopping were on colour. This led us to the next big discovery: we use simplified visual cues to recognize brands. For example, shoppers don't read "Diet Coke" on a pack when buying a two-litre bottle. They look at a brown liquid and a silver grey label and because they are in the context of the soft drinks category, they know that the brand is Diet Coke. We call this *colourshape*.

It is thought that at the beginning of a fixation the gist of the information is rapidly routed to a number of visual areas of the brain in a sweep that effectively says, "Does any part of the brain recognize this?" If any part of the brain does, then the information from the full fixation is routed to that part of the brain. This process is called *feedforward* and explains why colourshape is so important.

One of the fundamental challenges is that packaging designers and brand managers imagine that shoppers are reading when they shop. It has been thought that when we read, we understand by looking at the shape of each word. More recent research using eye-tracking has shown that when we look at (or more accurately fixate on) a word, usually toward the centre of the word, each fixation recognizes the shapes of the letters, its curves, horizontal and vertical lines, and then interprets and phonetically translates the meaning of these groupings into words. At the same time the brain is processing information from the periphery of the fovea, which is assessing the size of the next word and identifying the next fixation target, again usually to the left of centre of the new word. We often don't need to fixate on short words, conjunctions and prepositions such as "but", "and", or "to". It is by combining pattern recognition (letter shapes) and memory (learnt meanings) with the ability to predict from learning (context) that we understand what is written. This extract is popular and perhaps illustrates the point:

Olny srmat poelpe can raed tihs. i cdnuolt blveiee taht I cluod aulaclty uesdnatnrd waht I was rdanieg. The phaonmneal pweor of the hmuan-mnid, aoccdrnig to rscheearch at Cmabrigde Uinervtisy, it deosn't mttaer in waht oredr the ltteers in a wrod are, the olny iprmoatnt tihng is taht the frist and lsat ltteer be in the rghit pclae. The rset can be a taotl mses and you can sitll raed it wouthit a porbelm.

Shopping, however, is not reading. It is rarely an information-seeking exercise except when we go to research a complex new product or offer – for example, a new television. When we're grocery shopping we are following a learnt map around the store and using signpost brands to recognize categories. At that point, we switch from reflexive eye movement (fixating to interpret a scene) to attentional eye movement where we are actively seeking a learnt set of visual cues. This again uses pattern recognition (colourshape) as well as memory but there is little interpretation of the scene. While we may fixate on other parts of the category we are unlikely to process that information, because the task is one of seeking the learnt visual cues of the brand that we normally buy.

Human nature and the structure of many businesses reinforce the misconception that shoppers are reading and selecting instead of fixating and collecting. In a conventional brand manufacturer the brand manager, the person looking after the marketing of the brand, will typically be in the role for two or three years. How best for the new brand manager to make an impact and build their career? The most obvious step is to commission a redesign of the brand.

A very famous washing-up liquid brand went through this process. The brand manager's research told him that the design of the pack was unfeminine and outdated. The design agency was briefed to conduct a radical redesign of the pack. They changed everything: the shape, the colour and they made the packaging transparent so that you could see the product inside. They conducted focus groups and the feedback was fantastic. The new design was felt to be modern and feminine and everyone was reassured that consumers would definitely buy the repackaged product.

To great fanfare the new design was launched – and it flopped. It really bombed and sales plummeted. How could a new design receive such positive feedback and fail so badly? The answer is clear: washing-up liquid is a low interest category; people shop for it very quickly. Not only had shoppers learnt the colourshape cues for the old design, the retailers' private label products had also copied some elements of the old design. Shoppers running up to the fixture picked up what looked like their normal product and tossed it in the trolley. The brand had to put up pictures of the new and old design and say "If you used to buy this, it now looks like this" after losing a large amount of money.

Tropicana, the popular orange juice brand, went through the same process in the US in 2010. The new design was well-researched and although it played well with consumers it flopped with shoppers. They simply couldn't see it anymore because the simple visual cues that they had learnt about the brand were gone. The new designs had become gorillas. Shoppers were in the task of buying juice or washing-up liquid and there were some learnt visual cues associated with that task. Once these were removed, the product, although present on the shelf, became a black gorilla in a world of white T-shirted basketball throwers.

A friend of mine, Charlie Hiscocks, is an expert on global brands and he highlights the idea of fresh consistency. Maintaining the colourshape of a pack design does not mean that the design cannot be updated. He uses the example of James Bond. Several strong visual cues are associated with the James Bond "brand". A Caucasian male, 1.8 metres tall, in a black dinner suit with a pistol who at the start of each film turns to the camera, points his gun and fires. These images have allowed six different actors from 1962 to the present to play quite different interpretations of the James Bond character, and we believe that they are all James Bond.

Similarly, if you review the design of Heinz Cream of Tomato Soup from its launch in 1910 to the present day, the design is almost the same: the black tombstone shape, the red background and Heinz curved over the top of the tombstone. Marlboro, launched in 1924 with its iconic Red K-shaped pack top, has also changed little over its lifespan; the same is true of Coke's classic contoured bottle.

Not only do we learn the colourshape of packaging, we also learn other visual cues that help us shop. We learn the colourshape of the promotional material that the retailer uses, so much so that we will often just look at the colour and not read the promotion. This explains a recent study conducted in the US by Accenture where shoppers were interviewed as they left the store. The researchers identified all the products that had been bought that were on special offer, yet the shopper was unaware of more than half of the purchases being promotions!

We learn that the shelves on the end of the aisle, the gondola ends, are where the retailers do the big promotions. We've learnt it so well that again, we often don't read what the promotion is. We filmed shoppers buying from a gondola end that had an offer of buy one get one free. Around 80 per cent of the shoppers picked up only one product.

It is estimated that the grocery industry, including retailers and manufacturers, spend around $14 billion on point-of-sale (POS) around the world. Our conservative estimate is that 80 per cent is a waste of money due to three factors: location, content and format.

With great fanfare, several major retailers launched in-store television as an advertising medium in the early 2000s. Most of the operators focused on the fact that large populations came into their stores every day, giving brands much bigger potential audiences than the declining numbers they found on mainstream advertising channels such as television. The rate card, the amount that the retailers were proposing to charge for advertising on the screens in-store, matched that of national television and was therefore expensive. We were asked by one major brand to find out whether this new medium was effective. The particular retailer where we conducted some simple research had installed 55 large, flat-panel televisions all around a large superstore. At the entrance, suspended above the door was a huge flat-panel screen around two metres wide.

We stopped shoppers as they left the store to ask about the impact of the screens. After a very short introduction where we asked about their shopping mission and a bit of demographic information, our first question was, "Did you notice any television screens in the store today?" We asked 100, then 200, then 300 people. Only *two* shoppers could recall possibly seeing a television, and neither could remember what they saw on them. There were 55 massive television screens and yet nobody was noticing them.

The installation had failed, as with most of the others that we researched, because they were hung above the fixture and their location was wrong. Shoppers don't walk around looking up at the ceiling; unsurprisingly, their attention is taken up by the products on the shelves.

Many retailers in just about every part of the retail sector use hanging signs to promote offers or show lifestyle shots of their products being used. This represents a large cost expenditure and effort – these things have to be hung from the ceiling! We mentioned earlier in Chapter Three the problem of trying to communicate with shoppers in the car park as they arrived at the store. As part of this same study we continued in-store, again using shoppers wearing eye-tracking technology as well as then showing the shoppers footage of their own eye-tracks. We also used exit interviews with other shoppers to look at the relative performance of POS in the store. The shoppers we were interviewing and assessing used the non-food area of the store and also shopped in the aisles and walkways. We consistently found that well over 80 per cent of the fixations were on products and around ten per cent were on POS. The vast majority of these POS fixations were on the shelf around the product. Only a tiny proportion of fixations were on the hanging signs, yet that was where whole campaigns were being conducted. Again, the task of the shopper is to buy products, not read signs, particularly signs located above their heads. Location, location, location.

It is quite common for brands to offer gifts with purchases and we were asked by Coca-Cola to research the power of a promotion that they were about to run offering Coke drinking glasses. We were to test different locations for the POS but the content of the posters would be the same: a picture of the Coke glasses and the Coke product that shoppers had to buy in order to get them, including detailed instructions. The brand manager discussed with us how popular the real Coke glasses were with consumers and was very confident of the success of the promotion.

The displays were set up in three different convenience stores, each with the product and posters in different locations, and we recruited shoppers outside the store to wear the eye-tracker and shop as they would normally. When we interviewed shoppers as they left the store they all agreed with the brand manager that the offer of free Coke glasses would be very appealing. Some of the shoppers had noticed a Coke display; some people had even picked up products from the promotional display, and most had fixated on the poster. But no one could actually recall the offer.

Unilever funded a study into POS usage in hypermarkets in the UK and Thailand. In both countries there was *floor media* – a term for large posters stuck onto the floor of the hypermarket promoting brands and deals. As we will see later, humans naturally look downwards so these were expected to be successful. One of the floor posters we assessed was for a newly-launched dairy product that had won 11 prizes from women's magazines. The design of the poster had a picture of the product, images of the prizes it had won and several lines about the product that had helped achieve those wins.

Again, a few people fixated on the poster but there was no recall. For both Coke and the dairy product the locations made sense: they were where shoppers could see them. The reason they failed was because the content was so complex. In general, posters attract only around two fixations, so shoppers could not decode what the posters were about in the time they had. For convenience store shoppers most missions are very time-constrained; an important aim is to complete the shopping as quickly as possible and shoppers are therefore very focused on just doing the things that they came in to do. Any complicated messages have no chance of being read. This was the problem for the dairy product poster. It revealed a proud brand manager with all the awards that the product had won, and this was then combined with selling messages that were believed to influence consumers. Also, since the posters were on the floor and shoppers are moving, if they do fixate there will only be time for one fixation, so anything that does not have a very recognizable colourshape will not work.

We were asked by Diageo, a drinks company, to look at the various branded POS materials that they gave to bars and pubs. This included A-frames outside the bar, the illuminated bus stop signs we discussed before, posters to go on the walls, drip trays and bar mats, the fount at the bar and place mats for the tables. We thought this research would be interesting because shoppers here are generally the consumers and they would typically be spending a longer period of time in a relaxed frame of mind (at least, more relaxed than the convenience store shopper on a mission). One question we wanted to resolve was whether this meant that the branding would be more effective?

Of course, just as with supermarkets and fashion stores, there are still shopping missions in pubs, but they are simply different types of mission. They could be a regular meeting with friends, a big night out, a post-work quick drink, etc. All of these missions would create different mindsets and therefore different decisions needing to be made. We found that around one-third of shoppers didn't have a particular drink in mind before they came to the outlet. So, how did the different POS materials perform? We saw the same behaviour as with the stores: a person arrived at the outlet ignoring the POS outside as their task was to get into the pub. Then shoppers looked for the bar and as they approached, their focus was on locating the bar staff and finding the best place to stand to get served. We saw that shoppers who used the pub regularly would go to their normal places at the bar, and because they were familiar with the environment, ignore all the "wallpaper" (our POS materials) and just focus on the fount to make their final choice.

We found that those shoppers who were either in a group or unfamiliar with the environment were, like our supermarket car park shoppers, mentally preparing for the task ahead – that is, ordering their drinks. This meant that they were also focused on finding the best place to stand and there was actually more pressure on getting the decision right than in a self-service environment as they needed to know what they were going to order and also ask someone for the product that they wanted. Crucially, it is during this journey to the bar that most people make up their minds about what drink to order. While these shoppers were more likely than the regulars to look around, they were mostly looking at the bar staff, the founts and back of the bar and ignoring the drip trays and mats. Only once they had their drinks and sat down did these shoppers fixate on the mats, but very rarely did these fixations result in any recall. Now the shopper's focus was on consuming, relaxing and talking with their companions.

With this clear understanding of shoppers' behaviour Diageo then developed new materials that were used around the fount and at the back bar. After further research that confirmed the success of these new materials, Diageo reviewed the range of POS materials that they were providing for their outlets. By understanding what customers see and how they think, they was able both to sell more *and save* £5 million (around $8 million), simply by removing ineffective POS materials. This project and many others show that instead of trying to get as much POS into an outlet, such as a bar or store, brands are much more likely to succeed by focusing on a few simple items of POS and by reducing the clutter. This is much more likely to get through to the mind of a busy shopper.

The next chapter looks at the next stage of shopping: the deceptively simple task of actually choosing and buying something. It explains why it is often so difficult for stores to convert shoppers into purchasers and it looks at the surprising impact of categories and the power of scripted behaviour.

6

Buying It

"I always say shopping is cheaper than a psychiatrist."
Tammy Faye Bakker

I spent a very happy year working at Next for Men on London's Regent Street. At that time, in the mid-1980s, Next was a relatively new store that was experimenting with a different approach to displaying their clothes by grouping various products together into themes. This contrasted with the traditional approach that involved displaying all the trousers together in a single section, all the shirts in another, etc. The intention was to help shoppers build a total look rather than just choose the right shirt. This way the store would not only make shopping easier for their customers but also potentially sell more clothes.

I was responsible for the suits area, which included a made-to-measure offer. The front suit on the hanger faced out to the customer and was displayed with a shirt and tie, with the result that we often sold these "sets". This was something of a revolution in product display and contributed to Next's success, growing from 50 stores in 1982 to over 400 by 1988. About ten years after my experience of selling at Next, I was asked to research how people actually shopped in fashion stores. One of the first findings was that less than 20 per cent of shoppers actually bought anything; in fact, a high proportion of those who entered a store with the intention of buying actually walked out empty-handed.

Using a combination of filming and eye-tracking, we set to work exploring why these stores were so unsuccessful in converting shoppers into customers. Aside from the different colours and finishes that fashion retailers use and, of course, the products they sell, the formula for selling is very consistent and similar, from the premium end of the market to the cheapest discounters. Products are mainly displayed on hangers on the wall and the shop floor or they are folded-up and displayed on shelves and tables on the wall and the shop floor.

Clearly, whoever invented the idea of showing products as they would appear in a wardrobe or a chest of drawers has little understanding of how shoppers like to shop. In truth, in many fashion outlets there is little attention paid to the way that the shopper will make their way around the store. Typically, if a shopper interacts with a garment (for example, touches or picks it up) three times and is not engaged then they will leave the store.

Our research posed a vital question relevant for all fashion retailers: why is it so difficult for stores to convert shoppers into purchasers? The answer lies in a clear understanding of the way people think and behave when they are in a store. Once in "shopping mode" the shopper will walk slowly towards and around the fixtures. Their eye movement is focused on looking for design features that prompt the next stage, touching. Our hypothesis is that the feel of the garment allows the shopper to visualize what it will feel like to wear and how it will hang. Most of this activity is unconscious. This means that traditional hanging or folded displays makes shopping very difficult, with products often hung side-on to the shopper so they can only see a small portion of the garment. If the garment is a suit, for example, then the shopper can only see part of the jacket and nothing of the trousers. If it is a dress, then we can only see part of a pattern or design with no concept about the shape of the dress. This is why wall-based merchandising works better: products are more visible as they are visually higher and often there will be a front-facing display so the shopper can see more of the product on display. This highlights the first reason why fashion stores don't manage to persuade many shoppers to buy: the products on the display are at least partially hidden.

The second reason is that in most outlets fewer than half of the shoppers will talk to a member of staff and of those who do, the customer initiates around half of these conversations. Often the staff-led interactions are at the wrong time, before the shopper has found a product that they like, so the introduction is rejected. The key is to persuade the shopper to use the changing room, but here again we lose the shopper. Suppose I try on a pair of jeans and find that they are too small. Am I really likely to put my street clothes back on, hunt for the right size and then go through the process again? So unless the sales person follows up the visit to the changing room at the right time, another sale is lost.

As we saw earlier in Chapter Two, we shop in very different ways depending on the store we visit, the mission that we are on and the level of involvement we have with the items that we buy. Generally, the clothing purchase is one with high interest, high involvement and strong emotional content. Clothes are our own highly personal advertising, explaining who we are. Even those people who express no interest in fashion or what they look like will find that their clothes convey a message of their own.

This highlights an interesting concept in retailing: the power and relevance of *categories* of product. The significance of this concept was highlighted when we conducted some experimental work with Neil Munro of Unilever. As Unilever has brands in so many different categories, Neil was interested in the behaviours that occurred when people shopped across different categories. Unilever were keen to identify the key factors that influence the style of these shopping behaviours. What factors do people take into account for each category? What is the most significant mission for each category and what is the frequency of purchase? Other questions included: what decides whether a product is normally bought in the same store, how long do shoppers spend buying from the category, what proportion of those who start shopping go on to purchase, how does the outcome relate to the planned purchase, do shoppers always know which brand they are going to buy, what is the impact of promotions, what is the level of interaction with brands. After some experimentation it became apparent that two major factors were important: the shopper's level of engagement in decision-making and how often they repeated their purchase.

This meant that in some categories (for example, champagne), shoppers were more likely to make complicated decisions driven by the price of the product, their unfamiliarity with how to choose it and, for most shoppers, a low frequency of purchase. Other categories (such as milk) involved very simple decision-making, if any at all, and a high frequency of purchase. In the middle were categories like pet food, bought frequently but with some degree of decision-making, and household cleaning products, again with some degree of decision-making though more infrequently purchased. After mapping all the categories in the store it became clear that these different behaviours had significant implications.

In categories such as milk, shoppers almost always purchased the same product, so they were merely looking for simple visual cues to find it. The requirement for this type of category is therefore, simplicity of merchandising. Help the shopper get in and out of the category as swiftly as possible and do not confuse the process with POS materials or a bewildering array of different options. This contrasted with the champagne-style category, where the shopper would spend a long time considering different options. In this situation extra information, a varied or complex assortment and even educational promotions would be appropriate.

This helped us understand some of the successes and failures of in-store activity that we had seen. Some years ago, perhaps based on the mistaken idea that the categories are impulsive, one of the major supermarkets created a "snack and pop" decorative area for soft drinks and crisps. There were lots of colourful, cartoony display graphics around the products – and the concept failed. Both of those categories are in the "milk" segment: products bought frequently with little decision-making. As a result, making the shopping process more distracting with graphics is off-putting. Asda, another of the UK's largest supermarkets, went the opposite direction, choosing to simplify the soft drinks range, showing a reduced number of options in big brand blocks and, as a result, making the fixture extremely easy to shop. This approach triumphed.

Most of the categories in the grocery store can be mapped in either the milk or pet food areas, with varying levels of frequency. This has some interesting implications. First, we discussed in the previous chapter the role of the signpost brand in identifying the category and in preparing people to shop. Given that so many of the categories we buy tend to involve little decision-making, only a small amount of time is given to shopping these categories – often less than 45 seconds (it takes about 30 seconds to walk down an aisle without doing anything). So, faced with a complex range of categories with up to 200 differing options, how will shoppers find the colourshape of the brand that they normally buy so efficiently?

The answer lies in our ability to short-cut conscious behaviours, something that goes beyond our ability to recognize patterns and link those patterns to meanings. For example, think about driving a car. When red lights show on the back of the car in front, you don't need to think about what to do, you have learnt to also apply the brakes yourself. This is a *behavioural script*. When you approach a door, not only have you learnt that there is a usual place to look for a handle, you have learnt a script as to how to operate it. This applies to our knowledge of the store. Operating with the cognitive map of the geography of the store, coupled with the signpost brands triggering recognition of the categories, are often learnt scripts of behaviour associated with that category.

This might be a very simple script of learning where the brand you always buy is located on the shelf. We were asked by Nestlé to study how shoppers used the hot beverages category of tea and coffee in superstores. The category was more likely to be purchased as part of a main shopping mission and about one-third of shoppers bought the category every week from the particular store we surveyed. The majority of those that we interviewed after they finished shopping for coffee said that they intended to come to the category. A sizeable number already knew which specific brand and size they were going to buy. This suggests a high level of scripted behaviour; the average time that was spent shopping the category was just 12 seconds and shoppers rarely moved out of the selection of "my brand". A large number of shoppers didn't even actually shop; they had learnt the location of their choice so well that they simply reached out their hands and picked up the product with barely a glance at the shelf whilst still moving.

For SAB Miller, one of the world's largest brewing businesses, we researched the beer category in South Africa, investigating how shoppers bought beer in walk-in fridges. For the first time ever we saw 100 per cent of shoppers having a pre-determined brand and 98 per cent of them completing that purchase. Being regular shoppers, they rushed into the fridge area where they knew their product was located, grabbed it and left. Is it that South Africans are particularly or unusually loyal? No, this was scripted behaviour created by an uncomfortable environment. Instead of the kind of browsing that we would expect from such a high interest category, the shopper was motivated to stick to a predetermined choice by the fact that the display area was uncomfortably cold.

Scripted behaviour can be more complex. We studied European shoppers buying deodorants. Shoppers again were very clear about what they were going to buy, nearly all knew what brand to buy, but some of them were then going to make a fragrance choice once they got to the fixture. This decision was made quickly: shopping for the item took 16 seconds and one shopper in five tested the product before buying. Here, the learnt script includes testing the product. We even saw a few shoppers actually putting the roll-on under their arms – so, when you next buy deodorant you might want to choose the second one back on the shelf!

Contrast this behaviour with shoppers buying herbs and spices. The owners of the Schwartz brand were interested in making sure that the display was as easy as possible to shop, so we filmed and interviewed shoppers in a superstore to find out. Unsurprisingly, people didn't shop this fixture that often, two-thirds of those who we asked visited the fixture once a month or less. The purchase tended to be heavily planned, with most people stocking up and a few shopping to fulfil a specific recipe. Despite all this preparation, it took over a minute to browse the fixture; some of that time was spent just studying the display and around 30 seconds, interacting with the product. There was much reading, either on shelf or in the hand, more than you would see in wine. And despite everyone knowing what they wanted before they got there, nearly two shoppers in ten failed to buy. So, without a learnt script of behaviour, combined with lots of similar-looking products, shoppers found the fixture off-putting and many ended up walking away, unable to find the product they had wanted. So Schwartz redesigned everything, packaging and display, so that when we went back and researched the changes, shoppers found the display much easier to shop.

We have filmed and observed shoppers in just about every category in the store and in most countries around the world. In markets where shoppers have had the benefit of modern superstores for longer, we see more scripted behaviour. In markets where this style of shopping is new, we see quite different behaviour. For instance, I was watching shoppers in the Co-op Mart in Vietnam and was amazed to see that for almost every category, shoppers were picking up products and reading them, partly because they were learning about the brands, and partly because they were suspicious about where the product had been made. The milk scandal in China in 2008, which affected around 300,000 babies and killed six, had made Vietnamese shoppers very wary.

One clear implication of scripted behaviour is that trying to change the shopper's "usual" choice is going to be difficult. One of the most heavily scripted categories is tobacco – shoppers buy the category very frequently, often from the same outlet and are extraordinarily loyal to their brands. Even here, however, long-term changes can be made. A core activity for brand managers is to encourage consumers to switch brands. One tobacco brand has been particularly successful in achieving this by taking advantage of scripted behaviour. The main brand they were targeting was much larger in terms of market share. The challenger began by persuading retailers to change the way that the tobacco fixture was displayed, so that their brand was located next to the main brand. Shoppers look at the fixture as part of their learnt script to make sure that their brand is there before they ask for it. By being more visible, the challenger not only increased brand awareness but because the brands were next to each other, shoppers assumed that they were similar. As a result, the challenger brand was able to "steal" some of the main brand's value. Over time, sales of the challenger brand increased significantly.

This scripting occurs in all sorts of retail sectors. Working with McDonald's, we used eye-tracking techniques, this time to discover how shoppers used the restaurant to find the meal they wanted. Well over half of McDonald's shoppers return at least once a week, so are familiar with the fast-food process and, in all likelihood, their particular branch. McDonald's likes to suggest meal ideas to shoppers as they approach the restaurant and from the door to the counter, using window posters and hanging signs. The most common behavioural script is to look through the window to see how busy the outlet is, and then to focus once through the door while getting to the counter. That means that window posters and hanging signs are ignored.

This leads to another question: if shoppers have learnt where to find their brand on the shelf or in the store or restaurant, does this mean that there are no highly visible areas on the fixture? The answer is no: there are visible areas, and while behaviour may be heavily scripted there will always be shoppers who for a variety of reasons, decide to change brands. Also, there will always be new shoppers coming into the market, even for categories like toilet rolls that are bought by nearly every household (nobody has ever adequately explained to me what happens in the three per cent of households that don't buy toilet rolls in the UK).

Visibility in the category is still important and there are several factors at play here. First, there is the signpost brand. Because shoppers will tend to look here first there is a "visual halo" around that brand – it is the place that shoppers are likely to see first – so it will often be one of the strongest locations. Other issues are relevant as well. When I first started working with brands in grocery I kept hearing the mantra

"eye-level is buy level". This meant that eye-level was the b
on which to have your brands displayed. As a result, brand
pay the retailer what is called a higher listing fee to get onto that
shelf.

One of the first big brands with which we used eye-tracking was
very interested in the effect of this eye-level shelf. The assumption
was that "eye-level" was level with the height of the eyes – for the
average European female as the target shopper this would be about
1.6 metres high. The business that we were working with, Procter
& Gamble, sold a wide range of brands in a variety of categories,
with the result that they spent significant sums of money on listing
fees. The results were great news for the brand. We discovered that
humans look between 15 and 30 degrees downwards, which meant
that eye-level was actually lower by one shelf than the main one
that the retailers were charging for. There was much puzzlement the
following year when brands went in to negotiate their listings and
asked for a cheaper shelf, perfectly happy to let their competitors
have what was previously considered the "right" one. (The main
reason that we look downward relates to the weight and shape of our
head and the way it is balanced on our necks.)

Another myth that has been dispelled by observing shoppers in action
is the concept of "first in flow". It seemed to make sense, figured the
brands and retailers, that the first thing shoppers would see as they
approached the aisle was the first bay, meaning this would be the most
visible position in which to place your products. As we conducted
more eye-tracking studies, we found that this concept broke down,
something that was obscured until the advent of eye-tracking.

During the same study for Unilever that took place in three
hypermarkets, one in Thailand and two in the United Kingdom, Neil
asked us to use the eye-tracker, not only to understand how shoppers
used POS materials in-store but also to look at how shoppers
navigated around the store. As shoppers approach an aisle they are
in location mode in either the cross break or top break, much as we
discussed in Chapter Three. This means they are then side on to the
aisle and as the entrance opens up, the shopper looks into the aisle

towards the centre to see what category is located there, again often fixating on the signpost brand to help with recognition. If the category is one that the shopper wants to visit, they turn into the aisle or, more likely, manoeuvre the trolley in. This physical activity will pull eye movement very low, often around floor height.

The shopper is switching from location mode into shopping mode, triggering the script of how they normally behave in that aisle. By this time, the shopper is usually one or two metres into the aisle and their eye-level rises. They are prepared to shop the category. Of course, this means that they have already passed the first bay of the aisle and are unlikely to return to it. A combination of the perspective of looking down the aisle, the location of the signpost brand and eye-level all go into creating a diamond shaped hot spot. This is usually centred on the signpost brand and the largest vertical point of the diamond. The horizontal width of the diamond then spreads out from the signpost, getting narrower towards either end of the category.

This increased understanding of how we shop in categories raises another interesting question: if most categories are heavily planned, with shoppers knowing what they buy as part of their learnt script of behaviour, what role then does price play? Price is the focus of most of the negotiations between retailers and manufacturers, and when you ask shoppers they will often say that price is an important, if not the most important, reason behind their choice of a particular product.

Without doubt, most shoppers are aware of the overall cost of their shopping basket, particularly relating to their big weekly shop. We continuously hear about price wars between the retailers and it's certainly the case that in markets where most shoppers are poor, price is very obviously part of the shopping process. Studying shoppers in hard discounters, you will often see shoppers using a calculator to keep a running total of what they are spending.

The impact of price, however, may be more an issue of perception than reality. We featured in a television programme recently where the makers were interested in how shoppers considered prices in-store. They asked a shopper to come to her familiar store on the outskirts of East London and we equipped her with the eye-tracker. When she was interviewed by the presenter, she described herself as a savvy shopper, always careful with what she was buying and keeping a close eye on the prices of all the products that she bought. She was therefore stunned to discover that she only looked at a price label twice during the 30 minutes that she was shopping!

It's worth spending a moment to think about whether pricing – supposedly so important to so many consumers – is an issue of perception or reality. If I ask you how important prices are when buying your weekly groceries, then I can almost guarantee that you will tell me they are very important, if not the most important factor. Next time you go shopping for food try to keep an eye on whether (or how often) you look at prices. If you do, it is more likely to happen either in those categories that you shop very infrequently or in those categories where the item is notably more expensive. We also sometimes use price to help us categorise our choices and the wine category is a good example of this.

Most wine buyers in the UK and US are inexperienced. It is a category with very few "leader" brands to help guide and influence the shopper. As a result, people don't have many decision-making criteria to help them choose, except that they have probably tried something before and found it broadly acceptable. So the typical wine shopper finds an area of likely choice, say red and French, then uses prices to group the options into a smaller selection. In the end, the final choice is often an attractive label.

Much academic work (including price testing) is done in laboratory conditions, asking shoppers away from the store whether they would buy certain products at varying prices. Given the range of other factors that influence shoppers, primarily habit, these trials provide questionable results at best. This is because they are forcing shoppers to make conscious choices when in reality shoppers are much more likely to do things unconsciously. Price changes obviously affect behaviour, particularly for large brands, but the more interesting question is, who is it exactly that is responding to the changes?

The reason that we don't look at price labels is often because of the force of habituation. Every time you approach a fixture to shop the category you buy every week with your usual brand preference, you behave differently to the way you did when you *first* decided to buy that brand. In the beginning, there might have been some rational decision-making that may well have included a price comparison (more about this later). However, once your choice is habitual, why would you repeat the whole decision making process? It would be an inefficient use of scarce time. In the next chapter, we consider the vital issue of habituation – how we form habits and what this means for our behaviour when we're shopping – in greater detail.

7 | Habituation

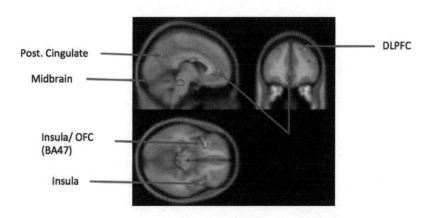

Post. Cingulate

Midbrain

Insula/ OFC
(BA47)

Insula

DLPFC

*"Curious things, habits. People themselves
never knew they had them."*
Agatha Christie

Take a look in your kitchen and bathroom cupboards and examine the brands inside. What do you notice about them? All look pretty familiar? When discussing grocery brands in focus groups, consumers often describe how they are always on the lookout for new brands to try. That's part of the reason why the Fast Moving Consumer Goods (FMCG) industry invests billions of dollars in designing and developing them. As we mentioned before, despite this apparent demand and fervent, sustained effort by the brands, globally, an incredible 80 per cent of new products fail within the first three years.

The reason for this failure can be found in your cupboards. Part of the reason why the brands in your home look so familiar is because they are exactly that: they are the brands that you buy every time. People typically buy the same brand of coffee, ketchup, washing-up liquid, washing powder and so on. Similarly, if we look in your wardrobe we might well find repetition in the clothing brands you wear, particularly if you are over 35.

Take any of the grocery brands that you buy again and again. Why do you buy this one? Is it really that much better? Have you tried all the alternatives? How did you decide that it was better? If, for example, it is the brand that you use for washing clothes, not many of us are qualified to examine the true performance of a detergent in removing visible and invisible elements that dirty our clothes or in conducting reviews across all types of fibres. Often, it is the brand that seems to suit us best and do the job well enough that we end up buying regularly.

I first started wondering about this when studying two rather intimate product categories. The first was bras. We discovered that well over two-thirds of British women bought the wrong size bra, usually one that was too small. The second was sanitary products. We noticed that shoppers picked out their items very quickly, understandably slightly embarrassed about being seen buying in that category. But what was amazing was that when we really questioned women of all ages about the brand and type of product they used, they talked about continuing to buy the same brand that their mothers had originally purchased for them, often the wrong one for their particular needs. This leads to a simple and fundamental question: how could this happen?

First, we find that for most shoppers in most categories, the brand that "sort of does the job" is acceptable. This is because initially, we don't want to dedicate too much time researching which brand to choose, and we certainly don't want to go through some kind of comparative trading-off of product attributes against cost every time we make a regular purchase. Second, most of these categories aren't actually that important to us in the overall scheme of our lives. Yes, when we go to buy a new car, television or camera we are likely to go online, find comparison sites, read reviews and take advice from friends and family. We will go to the store and assess the options, go away, probably go online again, read more reviews, consider the pricing options and finally make a decision about whether and what to buy. If most of us had a spare week or two to review the 150 – 200 products that we regularly buy, then maybe, just maybe, we might go through this process. But would we do this every time we buy household cleaners, or salt or pet food? Of course not; life's too short.

Unfortunately, there has been some misleading research that considers the key question of how we make decisions. People have discussed the question that I asked at the beginning of the chapter in focus groups – how did you decide to buy product x – and you become aware of the amazing post-hoc justification for the decision. Most shoppers don't want to sound like they are imprudent household managers, so will beef up the process that they went through in making their choice and deliver a rational, step-by-step series of decision-making and justifications to the researcher. These are called decision trees, and the research industry has tried to tell us that this is how shoppers make decisions, usually in five or six stages.

Let's take soft drinks as an example. The decision tree here is believed to look like this: first choice, which subcategory (for example, colas, flavoured carbonated drinks, etc); second choice, whether to opt for a brand or a private label; third choice, pack size; fourth, flavour; fifth, price. The brands have then planned their activities thinking that this happens every time a shopper comes to the fixture. If that were true, it would take around 14 hours to get through your weekly shopping.

Clearly this does not happen every time we go shopping. Kantar Worldpanel is a research business that specializes in running very large research programmes where they ask thousands of shoppers to keep a record of all the food and drink products that they buy. In the UK, for example, there are 21,000 households from a representative cross-section of British society who keep the receipts of all the products that they buy and then scan them every time they come home. This forms a vast database of what people are buying, where they are buying it and what sort of shopping mission they were on, from buying a can of Coke in a convenience store to completing the big weekly shop at their supermarket.

To investigate what is really happening I asked a question of Phil Dorsett at Worldpanel: how often do we really make a repeat purchase of the same brand? Using his vast set of data he confirmed that 55 per cent of shoppers buy the same brand when they make a repeat purchase in a category. When shoppers are on a large main shopping mission, 69 per cent of repeat category purchases are the same brand.

For low-involvement categories – those categories that we shop for quickly and are perhaps not that interested in – 69 per cent are repeat brand purchases.

Interestingly, it is not just brands that become habits when we shop. We can train people to become habituated to promotions. For example in the UK, beer has been a category with a disproportionate number of major promotions for many years. Shoppers have been trained to buy the promotions rather than simply buy a unit of their favourite brand. Instead of favouring a single brand, most shoppers will feel that four or five brands are acceptable and will buy the one that is most aggressively promoted. In these categories, only 51 per cent of purchases will be brand repeats.

It is not just the brands that we buy habitually. Consider another question: how inventive are you in the kitchen? Sadly, Britain does not have a world-renowned reputation for its food culture; in fact, as I travel around the world, the dish I see presented in hotels and restaurants to represent British cuisine is fish and chips. So perhaps you will be unsurprised that the average British household rotates just *eight* meals. I was shocked when I first heard this fact; I considered myself at least a "weekend chef" with an interest in food. However, when I reviewed our household meals, the repeated rotation of the same items was pretty familiar. What about the French? They have an extraordinary reputation around the world for their food cuisine. Another shock – it was much the same story. When we review the top 15 meals consumed in the UK 15 years ago versus today, the list is almost exactly the same, only the order of the list has changed.

Research published in 2006 suggests that we have evolved to be habitual. By analyzing how people's brains work while gambling, the team led by Dr Nathaniel Daw and Dr John O'Doherty at the UCL Gatsby Computational Neuroscience Unit found that trying out new things uses high-level regions of the brain, whereas falling back on familiar territory involves areas of the brain associated with reward and pleasure. This brain activity may reflect the fact that exploring new options requires us to override the desire for immediate profit, a cautious response that may be evolutionary. Preferring a known food source and avoiding the desire to gamble on trying a new one could have been critical to our survival.

As we have already seen in Chapter Five, our ability to recognize patterns and ascribe values to them shows that we are brilliant at learning things and that we potentially use shortcuts to recognize them. Again, it makes evolutionary sense that once we have made a decision about something that is at best, mildly important to us, we don't then waste our attention and energy by continually reassessing that choice. The task or chore of grocery shopping is made easier by all these habitual choices. We can rely on the behavioural script that we have learnt to lead us to the brand that we normally buy; because of this, we do not need to waste our effort and attention in finding it.

This leads to two further questions: how powerful is this habit? What kind of commitment do we have to this habit? Just because a person appears loyal to a brand (for example, flying with the same airline again and again) it doesn't mean they're committed to it. They may simply be using it out of habit. Break the habit and there is no loyalty. When loyalty is based on commitment, however, it is much harder to break because of the emotional attachment.

While investigating these questions further I met with an interesting expert, Butch Rice, in a little restaurant in Paris. A larger than life character, Butch has a celebrated reputation as an innovator. In a warm and sunny courtyard, he told me the story of his business, Research Surveys, now part of TNS. After establishing one of the most successful research businesses in South Africa, Butch met an academic from the University of Cape Town, Jannie Hofmeyr, who commissioned some fieldwork from Butch's company. Their project began by exploring the idea of religious conversion. What creates commitment to a religion, and why is the process of conversion sometimes sudden and at other times more gradual? Jannie was developing theories and models for commitment and conversion and his work moved into politics just as South Africa was in the grip of a democratic revolution.

Together, Butch and Jannie developed a research process called the Conversion Model which is now used around the world. This process explores psychological commitment to a wide variety of brands, whether political parties, cars or supermarkets. The model uses four dimensions to measure commitment:

> *Satisfaction* – how pleased we are with our choice of brand.
>
> *Perception of the alternatives* – for example, we often stay with our own bank only because our perception of the alternatives is that they are all just as bad.
>
> *The importance of the brand choice* or, put another way, how involved the consumer is with the category in question.
>
> *Ambivalence* – the fact that alternatives are also attractive, so it is difficult to make a final decision.

Using very simple questioning, the Conversion Model can identify several groups of consumers and their respective levels of commitment to brands within a specific category. These initially split between brand users and non-users. Users range from individuals who are entrenched and committed to those who are convertible and uncommitted. Non-users includes those people who are open and available, those who are open and ambivalent, and those who are completely unavailable. These characteristics can be either imperceptible or strongly pronounced.

The implications of this for retailing are significant: it means that every category will have a mixture of shoppers who are committed and habitual in their choices, a group of people who are ready to be persuaded between a number of potential brand choices, and a further group of people who are either actively seeking to change their previously committed choice, or who don't really care about the brand they buy. This is important because the way that these shoppers will shop the category will differ. Some will simply look to activate their behavioural script and ignoring any other visual distractions, will focus attention on the colourshape of the brand that they normally buy. This contrasts with other shoppers who are perhaps more consciously making choices using the information that is presented to them, perhaps related to flavour, size or maybe even price. The implication is that the same group of products and the same display have quite different jobs to do.

This situation is reflected in the segmentation of categories that we have explored in the previous chapter. For categories like milk, purchased frequently and with little active decision-making, there is a tendency towards a high proportion of habituated shoppers. This contrasts with categories such as champagne, purchased infrequently and with a higher level of price and decision-making that tend to have a much higher share of *available* shoppers. How categories are presented – the assortment, the merchandising, information and communication, pricing and promotions – should all take into account the different levels of commitment and therefore, where the category segments.

Often we find that categories with a higher proportion of shoppers who don't really care about their brand choices are more sensitive to price changes (called price elasticity), while those with higher levels of habituation are less sensitive. This means that potentially, price changes are merely attracting non-loyal shoppers. Of course, this is fine, as long as the switch is permanent and not simply a permanent switch to whatever has the lowest price.

In the study run by Cristina de Balanzo, head of Neuroscience at TNS, Professor Gemma Calvert of Neurosense and Tim Ambler, Honourary Fellow at London Business School, we investigated the Conversion Model process. The commitment levels are measurable for several brain network responses. We investigated what happens in the brain when shoppers fixate on the brand that they most often purchased. As mentioned, the experiment combined fMRI with eye-tracking and when respondents came to the end of the film of the process of shopping the coffee and detergents fixtures, they selected their preferred brand. We had discovered their preference when we recruited them several weeks before. When these data were compared with a control test, the areas of the brain that were intensively active are those that prepare us for action, long-term memory and recall of associations, desirability, preference and perhaps most interestingly, reward.

What we are measuring using the Conversion Model technique is the brain's process of assessing levels of reward and recalling associations, as well as the brand's salience and our habitual responses.

Understandably, humans seek those things that provide pleasure and reject those that give pain. One aspect of our perceptions of brands is our recall associations that recollect degrees of reward.

A brand's salience or ability to influence is a combination of three factors, what T. H. Walvis from THEY, a Dutch brand management firm calls coherence, richness and relevance. Coherence is the degree of memory encoding, the repeated synaptic firings of the neuronal cloud. Richness is the variety of sources of those encodings. It is worth remembering that by experiencing the brand in many different scenarios we increase the interconnectedness of the memory. Relevance is simply the relevance of the brand to the task at hand. We have already seen how important the task is in the brain's use or rejection of information. Finally, the strength of our habitual responses depends on how often we repeat the task of choosing.

A popular scientific study exploring the issue of commitment was conducted by researchers at NYU led by Samuel McClure who used fMRI technology to demonstrate the effects of brand salience. They found that strong coherence, richness and relevance representation have the power to affect preference decisions. The study involved two types of tests: first, a behavioural preference test was conducted in which respondents took part in anonymous and semi-anonymous taste tests directly comparing the cola drinks Pepsi and Coca-Cola. The key finding from this test was the effect that brand knowledge has on preference decisions, particularly on Coca-Cola. It was found that respondents were far more likely to state that they preferred Coca-Cola when they drank it from a cup displaying the Coca-Cola logo than when presented with it unnamed. The knowledge that the cola being consumed was Coca-Cola significantly enhanced respondents' perceived enjoyment levels. Interestingly, this behaviour was absent when respondents performed the equivalent preference test for Pepsi from Pepsi labelled cups, suggesting that Coca-Cola is the more salient brand.

The second set of tests again used fMRI brain scanning equipment to monitor neurobiological activity whilst respondents performed similar preference tests. McClure and his colleagues found that fewer areas of the brain were active during the anonymous taste tests. The area of the brain associated with signalling basic aspects of reward was observed to be active during the anonymous taste tests. However, when respondents were provided with brand information (particularly when they thought they were drinking Coca-Cola) it was found that the areas associated with biasing behaviour were more active. Essentially, the presence of brand information has the effect of biasing individual preferences.

The study by Samuel McClure and his team is particularly interesting as it clearly explains the effect that brand cues can have on the shopper and consumer. In this case, visual cues relating to Coca-Cola had a significantly positive effect on the respondent's consumption experience, which was observed to be a result of the visual cues associated with Coca-Cola causing increased preferential neurobiological activity.

Does habit mean loyalty? The Ehrenberg-Bass Institute based at the University of Southern Australia also investigated the Kantar Worldpanel data that we mentioned earlier. Their particular focus was on consumers that are 100 per cent loyal to a brand. Common wisdom is that those who only buy one brand are the most desirable customers. After all, aren't their purchases more reliable and valuable? This leads to strategies to try to find or create more 100 per cent brand loyal buyers. However, empirical studies show that very few customers are 100 per cent brand loyal. Furthermore, those that are, tend to be low value consumers who buy less from the category. In other words, they have fewer chances to switch. Observing over time, we find the number of 100 per cent brand loyals declines as opportunities to buy from the category increase. For example, when researchers looked at buying habits in fast-food restaurants, 21 per cent of visitors were 100 per cent brand loyal over a four-week period, but when this was extended to three months, the proportion dropped to only 12 per cent. This natural trend to buy from more brands means that efforts to "convert" normal buyers to being 100 per cent loyal are likely to fail.

Phil Dorsett found that shoppers completing a small basket shopping mission were only likely to repeat purchase from the same category

51 per cent of the time. This suggests that where the priority for the shopping trip is time – that is, to find the products as quickly as possible – and when confused by overcomplicated merchandising or unavailability, people are more prepared to switch brands even though this is not necessarily easy. This highlights the fact that while we may prefer or even like the regular brands that we use, the idea of loyalty is relatively fragile. Perhaps it would be more useful to talk about the idea of habit and habituation rather than loyalty. Although this may seem semantic it could be significant in terms of how marketing develops and focuses its activities in the future. Perhaps instead of thinking of consumers' and shoppers' loyalty in the same way that a passionate football supporter might support Arsenal or Barcelona, we need to consider what constitutes habituation and habit in the context of washing powder and yoghurt.

Similarly, as we work to expand our business's market share it is worth asking what the competitive brands' habitual behaviours are and where can a marketer intervene? This leads to an understanding that in order to protect a brand's market share or take share from a competitor, the fundamental starting point for any marketing activity is rooted in the decisions that are made at the point of purchase by those shoppers that are habituated, available or floating. This understanding can then be used to potentially intervene in the choice-making process, whether via television advertising, promotions or other marketing activities.

It is worth explaining exactly what we mean by a brand's *mental* and *physical* availability, given their significance to the success of a brand. *Mental availability* (or brand salience) depends on the quality of branding and advertising, with distinctive, consistent icons and imagery building memory associations that allow the brand to be noticed and recalled across as wide a range of buying situations as possible. *Physical availability* simply means making the brand easy to notice and buy across as wide a range of buying situations as possible. This includes retail penetration and in-store presence.

Byron Sharp, writing in a paper for the Ehrenberg-Bass Institute, noted that brands compete largely in terms of their mental and physical availability. Brands that are better known and noticed by more people and brands that are more widely available, have greater market share. In fact, brands with a larger market share not only have greater physical and mental availability but also enjoy larger marketing budgets to support these assets. Buyers of one brand express much the same attitudes about that brand and their reasons for buying it as buyers of another brand. When buyers adopt a new brand their attitudes then change in favour of that brand. Crucially, brands within a product category sell to near identical consumers and each brand's consumer base differs from its competitors' chiefly in terms of size (numbers of buyers), not in demographics, psychographics, personality characteristics, values or attitudes. There is little evidence of brands being able to build special values that successfully differentiate (or insulate) them from their competitors. Buyers simply know and like the brands they buy, and they are vastly more likely to notice, consider and buy these brands over others.

These empirical patterns show that brands compete largely as branded versions of the product category. Even with their functional and image differences and, within limits, their different levels of price or quality level, there is little to differentiate them.

So, many brands are bought habitually and sometimes shoppers switch and potentially re-habituate to their new choice of brand. In some categories, and notably in high interest ones such as fashion, there is more active decision-making going on. This leads us to the question that we consider in the next chapter: how do we make decisions and choices when we are in a store?

8

A Matter of Choice

"All over the place, from popular culture to the propaganda system, there is constant pressure to make people feel that they are helpless, that the only role they can have is to ratify decisions and to consume."
Noam Chomsky

So far, we have seen how most of us shop regularly for groceries using familiar stores whose layouts we have come to learn. We have described the importance of the shopping mission when choosing which store to use, and how we often shop without a list but instead, use the store as a visual prompt to remind us of the things we need. The way that our brains work and the way we see have a huge impact on our ability to notice the things that the retailers and brand managers are trying to sell us. In fact, the mundane, routine task of finding the products that we want means we actually ignore most of what is around us. Instead, our visual search is guided by signpost brands that serve to introduce the category (such as soft drinks) and then stimulate a learnt behavioural script. We have discussed the importance of visual cues, notably a product's colour and shape, in helping us find the brand we want. Each category is shopped differently and our interaction is primarily driven by how much choice we need to make and how often we repeat this task in each particular category. We have also discussed how in many categories we tend to buy the same brands repeatedly.

All of these issues point to one unavoidable conclusion: most marketing is largely unsuccessful. Despite all the evidence and having access to most of this information, retailers and brand managers persist in using flawed business practices. As a result, they are wasting massive amounts of money that the consumer, you and I, eventually end up subsidising. The area of greatest waste is when marketers over-exaggerate the effectiveness of marketing activity, particularly advertising, before consumers become shoppers. This mistake is compounded by a lack of understanding of what actually happens when shoppers use stores. So much current marketing activity success hinges around the decisions that shoppers make in stores, yet so much of the reality of shopping is actually misunderstood. Instead, a better understanding of the process by which shoppers become consumers should drive all the activity that builds towards the sale. This process is such a vital, fundamental issue for anyone interested in retailing (including customers), that it deserves closer attention. So with all this habitual behaviour, what decisions are really being made? How do people think? How can they be influenced? While much of our discussion has been about grocery shopping it is also worth considering how decisions are made in retail sectors that we visit much less frequently, such as fashion, as well as those areas that are more complex, such as mobile phones.

Some of the most common questions that we ask shoppers after we have filmed them shopping in different categories is whether they had planned to visit the category today, whether they had planned to purchase, and whether they knew which brand they were going to buy before they reached the fixture. In the retail industry we talk about impulse purchasing, but true impulse purchasing – buying a category that you have never bought before – is actually very rare. We do, of course, buy things on semi-impulse. For example, seeing a category that is purchased either rarely or infrequently (like household cleaning), may trigger an unplanned purchase because shoppers are reminded that they are close to running out at home. This is particularly noticeable in a category such as batteries, where research suggests that the more battery fixtures there are in the store, within reason, the higher sales will be. Batteries are a classic example of a category that one plans to buy rarely and relatively infrequently, but actually most of us have some battery-operated machine at home that isn't currently working due to a flat battery. We just need to be reminded to replace it.

Levels of planned shopping vary and, interestingly, planning actually varies from country to country. In most European and North American markets, categories range from 60 – 95 per cent planned. In countries where shopping is evolving from daily purchasing to Euro-American levels we often see lower levels of planning. In Russia, for instance, there is around 20 per cent less planning. The nature of planning also varies, reflecting the levels of habituation. Heavily habituated categories, meaning those that are most frequently repeatedly purchased, usually show high levels of planning.

However, even in heavily habituated categories where shoppers repeatedly buy a planned brand with little decision-making, from time to time, other factors will stimulate a change. Research, again conducted by the Ehrenburg-Bass Institute, shows that around half of a brand's heavy users will not be purchasing that brand the following year. Several factors can prompt this change. For instance, if a desired brand is out of stock then shoppers clearly need to choose an alternative. It's worth noting that in heavily planned categories, although around one-third of shoppers claim that they would go to another store to buy the desired brand, this rarely happens. Certainly a shopper may defer their purchase to their next trip, but more commonly we usually have a small repertoire of acceptable brands and simply switch to that second choice.

In some categories, promotions can help prompt shoppers to switch brands, but in categories where there is always heavy promotional activity shoppers simply learn to look for promotions instead of brands. They will again have a repertoire of acceptable brands and just switch to whichever one is offering a deal. We see this is in categories like frozen food, particularly where the emotional link to the food is weaker (this is because the product is neither visible nor tactile). Promoting heavily is lazy retailing: it is easy to give products away, particularly when it is the brands that are being asked to fund the promotion. In a paper written in 2007, Rui Susan Huang and John Dawes examined the outcomes of 1,300 price promotions. In around half of the promotions, most of the volume that was sold would have sold anyway – shoppers would have bought the product whether or not there was a deal. This means that often a promotion costs the promoter more than what they make from the exercise: volumes may increase but not enough to offset the reduced margin.

Often a change of circumstances will prompt shoppers to reconsider their normal choice and review their repertoire. Clearly, circumstances change for many reasons, both major and minor. Major influences include the arrival of a baby, the departure of children or economic pressure such as a threat of job loss, while more minor factors include the opening of a shop that is closer and where there is reduced time pressure for shoppers.

Just occasionally, great marketing does manage to get through to shoppers and lead them to reconsider their normal brand choices. This might result from a major new television product launch, or a major new campaign supported with a big, in-store launch. However, great marketing that manages to fundamentally shift a shopper's behaviour is rare, despite the appropriately persuasive claims of marketers. It is a little like winning the lottery: everyone focuses on the possible upside (a win) while ignoring the reality of the situation for most people (no change or difference).

Until quite recently, most thinking about decision-making had been influenced by the 17th - century French philosopher Rene Descartes. In his series of writings called *Discourses*, Descartes provided a model for decision-making that separated the emotional approach from the rational. While developments in science have disproved some of Descartes' theories about how the brain works, the idea that humans make rational decisions unencumbered by emotions has lived on. This can be seen in a wide range of research studies where people are asked to rationally compare and trade-off different attributes so as to mimic the decisions leading to a purchase. More recently, however, a major breakthrough in neuroscience by Antonio Damasio in his book, *Descartes' Error,* develops the idea that emotions are unavoidably involved in *every* choice, and in fact they give value to the choices that we make.

It is worth pausing a moment to consider this issue in a little more depth. After all, the way the brain works is fundamentally important to the way we think and behave when shopping. There are three main functions operating in the brain: one is the *proto-reptilian* brain whose features we share with other mammals. This part of the brain is responsible for survival of the body, controlling heart rate and breathing as well as monitoring the health of the system – how hot, how cold and so on. The second part is the *limbic* or emotional brain, and the third is the *neocortex* or thinking brain.

Our eyes and vision processing send information to the limbic brain, where it interprets visual signals and prepares the body for action. The limbic brain is focusing attention and tagging whether the signal can be ignored. This is done by seeing whether it attracts a positive or negative emotional response. Joseph LeDoux, professor at the Centre for Neural Science at New York University, whose work focuses on the primary emotion of fear, describes what might happen during a country walk. The eyes fixate on something that looks like a snake. The visual signal passes through the limbic brain which attaches an emotion, a fear response, and an instruction to the neocortex to gather more information. With more processing we use the neuronal clouds in our memory to realize that it is just a stick and so the flight mechanisms in the body can be stood down. So the limbic system acts as an emotional thermometer, tagging all the sensory inputs as emotionally hot, cold or somewhere in between.

Also in the limbic system is a reward centre that monitors the response to stimulus; we learn things that give us pleasure and actively seek them out again. Of course, these pleasures are graded. The pleasure record of eating an ice cream, say, will rank differently to the pleasure record of successfully completing the washing up. The pleasure records are tagged with memories and associations in the neuronal cloud, and this in turn gives value to those memories. This process of seeking to repeat rewarding activities appears to be a fundamental part of our make-up and our emotional filtering of information, pain or reward, lies at the core of our decision-making. Damasio explains this situation in his *Somatic Markers* hypothesis. By using our experience of situations with their tagged emotional markers, we can immediately assess sensory inputs and either reject or act on them. This filter determines what we pay attention to and what we learn, and this combination of attention and memory affect how we perceive our world.

This is, of course, directly relevant to the world of brands and branding. One of the notable features of shopping is the point about impulse buying that we mentioned earlier. It is extremely rare that we purchase a category that we have never experienced before. This is not a decision to marry someone, or to travel somewhere completely unfamiliar on holiday. Generally, we are making in-store decisions using existing preferences and this can be seen repeatedly when we use an fMRI to examine neural activity. A study published by Brian Knutson from Stanford University and his team showed that when we make choices between products with very visible pricing, the part of the brain that anticipates gain and loss is activated, while other areas of the brain that are normally active in other types of decision-making, notably learning, are not.

So how have we developed these existing, well-established preferences? The answer is that we gather information about brands through a wide range of direct and indirect methods. Information is presented to us about brands through advertising but we also make assessments of brands through word of mouth, by seeing other people use the brand, by seeing the brand in the store and through many other, less-controlled ways.

When we watch advertising most of us tend to diminish our focus, usually giving less attention to the advert than to the programme we want to see. It is suggested that we typically don't process any information for about half of the adverts that we see, and that we are much more likely to give attention to advertising for brands that we already like and use. In a paper entitled *The hidden power of advertising*, Robert Heath, an advertising academic at Bath University, describes what happens when we watch a television advert. Good advertising not only grabs our attention and engages us, it also helps us to learn information about a brand; this, in turn, means that we can create what are called *analytical memories*.

If I interviewed you a week or so after and asked whether you had seen the ad and what you could remember, it would be the analytical memories that you would recall. However, at the same time as we are engaged in high attention processing, we are also receiving information from the advert using low attention processing. These are called *conceptual* or *perceptual* memories and they might include aspects such as colours related to a brand. Procter Gamble, owners of the Gillette brand, used both high and low attention thinking when they launched the Gillette Fusion brand.

As well as all the visual images that you often see with Gillette advertising – shots of razor blades, attractive men using the product, scientists at work – the adverts also feature the colours blue and orange in nearly every frame of the film. These colours are the palette of the brand. What the advert was designed to do was not only to create analytical memories, in this case about the number of blades and the involvement of scientists in the development of the product, but also to equip you with conceptual memories about the colour of the brand. This matters, because we have already seen how important colour is to in-store product recognition.

Building on Damasio's idea of somatic markers I believe that for each brand that we recognize we have an *Emotional Packet*, a loose collection of memories, emotions and sensations that have been learnt from a wide range of sources, including advertising and exposure to the brand, both in-store and elsewhere. We saw the existence of this emotional packet in our eye-tracking and fMRI study conducted on the coffee and detergents categories. Once respondents fixated on the brand that they bought most often, the areas of the brain that were notably active were in the part of the limbic brain that identifies reward, and the area that organizes the somatic marker.

Each shopper's emotional packet is determined by their needs from a particular category. As an example, consider the category of yoghurts. A consumer might want brands that offer great fruity taste and a healthy product in convenient packs. In reviewing the brands that are available, the shopper uses the emotional packet that he or she has learnt about each brand and then matches that against a particular core need from a category.

When a shopper moves away from their normal purchase and makes a choice, they are paying attention to the options that are visible. The emotional packet is of course, not fixed, which means that while conducting a split second review the shopper may process new information relating to a particular brand which will then affect that brand's emotional packet. This information might be processed in either high or low attention. For example, while reading a package the shopper may find some extra nutritional information that improves the emotional packet related to that brand. Similarly, a brand's location on a shelf and its proximity to another brand may unconsciously communicate significance about its value or status.

It appears that the stronger the emotional packet, the less likely the shopper is to be rational when finalizing their choice. For example, consider a shopper in a high-end fashion retailer such as Ralph Lauren. Rationally, we know that the T-shirts on sale cost only a small amount of money to produce. Yet because of the strength of the emotional packet for some shoppers, this rational fact is disregarded and the shopper will pay many times the manufacturing price.

Returning to the grocery store, we have another challenge to face when the shopper is making choices. For a brand to be considered, it first needs to be visible. In most categories in the store there are simply too many options for the shopper to review all of them, particularly in the limited time available. In most countries, there is a range of around 250,000 potential products available for a retailer to choose. Of these, a typical hypermarket stocks around 80,000 products. It is this enormous range that consumers highlight as one of the reasons they elect to go to these types of stores – precisely because they offer the convenience of a one-stop shop. The irony, however, is that the average developed market household will only use around 300 of these product options in a year, and only half of these, 150 or so, will be used regularly. So why is there such a large disconnect between the number of brands that the retailer believes he has to offer, and the number of brands that we actually choose? The answer is that retailers, when interviewing their customers, hear that they want choice. The assumption the retailer makes is that to provide customers with choice means stocking a vast range of options.

All of our research shows that it is impossible for us to review all the options that are available when we go grocery shopping. Yet if that is the case, what does the shopper actually want when they ask for "choice"? What they actually mean is "I want the right choice for me," which of course relates to a much smaller range of options. An example of what this means in practice was shown in a project for Danone, the dairy and water company. They conducted a review of the yoghurts category in an Italian retailer, evaluating the rate of sales of all the options that were on the shelf. They boldly recommended to the retailer that the range be cut by 40 per cent. This proposal was accepted and the shopper's conscious reaction was measured. Keeping in mind that nearly half of the options previously available had been removed, only 15 per cent of shoppers noticed anything different about the category; of those people who did notice a change, most thought that there were *more* options available. At the same time, sales were monitored and they increased by over 20 per cent. By offering too much choice, the range becomes invisible through complexity; by reducing range, options have the chance to become visible and therefore we see the actual choices.

There is another difficulty that arises when there is a complex range of products and little difference between them: *false memories*. In 1959, working in the University of Virginia's psychology department, James Deese conducted a study where he created lists of 12 associated words with a single critical word missing. For example, one list omitted the word "needle" but included the words thread, pin, eye, sewing, sharp, point, pricked, thimble, haystack, pain, hurt and injection. The researcher read the list to respondents and then asked them to write down what they could recall, starting with the last few words read out first, and then any others that they could recall with a strong degree of certainty. The result was that they were most likely to recall the words they heard both first and last. The students recalled the critical missing word (ie, "needle") with about the same success rate as with recalling those words listed in the middle.

The second task involved respondents working with longer lists. When asked to recall, they had to state whether they "remembered" (meaning they were able to relive the experience of seeing the word) or "knew" (they were sure of seeing the word but could not relive the experience). Those that recalled the critical word even though it was not present were much more likely to claim to have *remembered* rather than to have *known* they had seen the word before.

One theory is that false recognition responses become embedded when people make associations. For example, when they see a word such as "hot" they might think of an associated word like "cold". Others think that memory encoding and retrieval happens via a system in the brain where there are many simple but interconnected processing units. This would appear to be reinforced by the massive capability of the human brain for pattern recognition; it would therefore make sense that the brain would store things that look or behave the same way together. Another theory is that the ease with which someone can bring events to mind increases the probability that the person will attribute the experience to being a memory. So if people fluently recall and recognize the word "needle", and if this fluency allows them to imagine the word being read out by the questioner in the study, then they are more likely to claim that they heard the word being spoken.

Other research into false recognition has shown that it almost disappears when there are highly differentiated things to remember; only when you start to use things that are closely related do false associations begin to grow. This was highlighted to us during a study of shoppers buying frozen foods, when we found that 23 per cent of respondents had selected the wrong product; that is, a product not only different from what they intended, but also from what they thought they actually purchased. Thus, because of the similarity of the brands and products that were on offer, shoppers believed that they had purchased a brand, the "needle" that they had not purchased; instead, they had purchased something very similar, but not the same.

Millward Brown, the world's largest advertising research agency, tested an advert for Skoda cars that showed the car being "made" by bakers, who were making a cake in sections that they put together to create a car. As part of the test they eye-tracked respondents watching the advert. The film focused attention on a key point in the advert – on the Skoda badge, and the eye tracking showed every fixating heavily on it. Yet after watching, a large proportion ᴏ₁ watchers claimed that the advert was for Citroen. I would suggest that the shape of the car being shown was a small hatchback that people fluently recall and recognize as a Citroen (famous for small, quirky cars) leading to the false memory, in this case for the wrong brand. Anecdotally, I have often heard that good brand advertising benefits not only the target brand but also other associated brands in the category, probably precisely through this phenomenon of false memory.

In his book, *The Paradox of Choice,* Professor Barry Schwartz describes other implications of offering too much choice. One is disappointment: with all these options available, the shopper's expectations of finding a perfect match is enhanced and is then inevitably disappointed. With this disappointment also comes regret and the view that "surely with all this choice I should have done better". Another response is confusion. When there is too much choice the shopper is ill-equipped to review all the possible options. The result is paralysis and the response then becomes, "I don't want to make the wrong choice but I don't know how to make the right one."

As discussed earlier, our brains are only able to process around seven bits of visual information at any one time, each bit being a chunk of information, such as a word or a familiar unit of information. Once this limit is overloaded the brain simply stops processing information. People specializing in the science of decision-making believe that when shoppers try to choose from a large selection, they subconsciously create a small subset of brands that helps ease their cognitive effort and helps them make a quick decision.

Some retailers have focused on this as a point of difference. Stew Leonards in Connecticut carries a much reduced range when compared with similar sized stores. It is not by chance that this retailer has the highest sales in the world per square foot. My friend Herb Sorensen, also a long-time shopping researcher, talks about the idea of "the big head and the long tail". The *big head* is the three per cent of products that deliver two-thirds of a store's sales; these are the items that the shopper wants to buy. The long tail is the 50 per cent of items that deliver just seven per cent of a store's sales. Shoppers say that the reason they go to the store is for all that perceived choice.

Brands that are likely to be considered by shoppers are those that are both visible and have an emotional packet. Given that one of the best means to build an emotional packet comes from advertising, a strong relationship between the amount spent on advertising and market share is to be expected. So, too, is the fact that advertising focusing on brand feeling is more likely to succeed. Coca-Cola is a great example of a brand that has focused its marketing efforts on feeling and visibility. Its advertising is directed towards making consumers feel part of the brand with very simple messages, and its activity in-store is strongly focused on visibility. There are few convenience stores or forecourts around the world that do not feature a Coca-Cola branded soft drinks fridge.

Recent research conducted using eye-tracking suggests that visibility can be even more effective than the memory-based stimuli that a shopper may see before shopping outside of the store. In a large study in the US using 60 stores, researchers investigated the effect of a product's precise location on a shelf on sales. Locating products in the highest visibility area, at eye-level, had the greatest sales effect. Further eye-tracking research appears to show that when faced with a cluttered group of options, we are most likely to look towards the centre of that group.

One of my colleagues, Ranjiv Gill, has highlighted the results from eye-tracking studies that we conducted across six different categories. He reviewed the data from these different studies and found that the most visible brands were most likely to be recalled by shoppers and most likely to be purchased. Where there were brands in the category that were well known through external marketing, stronger emotional packets meant they were recognized more easily, with fewer fixations. Also, their enhanced visibility on the shelf meant that they were more likely to be purchased, particularly if their packaging was strong and if the external marketing highlighted some connection with the design of the packaging.

These factors are particularly important in supermarkets because we are reluctant to invest too much time in the process of shopping – something common for most categories. In these circumstances we are not really making decisions but simple marginal choices between brands that we already know, and to do this we use as many shortcuts as possible, both consciously and unconsciously. I am often asked "How can we interrupt the shopper?" in order to change a potential decision. My response is always "Don't". When we make marginal choices in low involvement and low interest situations, interruptions are disruptive and, at their worst, can stop the sale altogether. Any interventions that we make must help the shopper make those shortcuts, either by increasing the visibility of the limited brand set that is relevant to the shopper, or by introducing a simple idea that is relevant to the needs of the shopper at that time. From our eye-tracking research we know that the focus of the shopper's visual attention is on products, not on signs or advertising. Of the few pieces of point-of-sale material that the shopper uses, the vast majority are those located around the product on the shelf edge. So, if we understand the shortcuts of habituated and available shoppers, we can make the shopping process more efficient and therefore more successful, rather than leaving it to the shotgun approach that with luck, attaches to someone.

Kimberly Clark (KC), makers of paper products such as nappies and tissues, were one of the first brand manufacturers to invest heavily in virtual reality as a shopper research tool. In addition to building half a supermarket at their head office in Appleton, Wisconsin, they invested in a huge display facility that allowed the other half of the supermarket to be projected in virtual reality. This meant that they could experiment with different displays, new packaging and potentially new products, without having to physically make them. KC also invested heavily in backing a virtual reality software company called Red Dot, who worked with us to create the virtual reality testing station. This meant that we could recruit shoppers in malls who were then asked to go shopping virtually. Built into the testing station was eye-tracking equipment that allowed us to do all the research that we would normally do in-store in a virtual superstore.

Οne of the research projects that we conducted with KC was in the bathroom tissue category. Again, we asked shoppers to shop a number of categories including ours, before interviewing them to investigate their decision-making process. With the eye-tracking data we could directly compare what shoppers told us that they had done with what had actually happened. Shoppers claimed that they used overhead signs to find the category, whereas in reality, they used the products themselves to recognize the category, again using a signpost brand. Most shoppers knew what brand they were going to buy and we saw from the eye-tracking that, with a few fixations, the habituated shoppers used a combination of colour and name to recognize their brand. Both the habituated and available shoppers said that looking at the number of rolls and the price tag was an important part of the decision-making process. Added together, fewer than three per cent of fixations were on these elements.

Other senses can also potentially come into play. Researchers from the University of Leicester in the UK experimented with music in the wine category. Having placed two displays in the aisle, one with German wine and the other with French wine, they then played German oompah music for a number of days, followed by some French music. Shoppers were attracted to and selected from the wine display that matched the musical stimulus.

There has also been experimentation with the sense of smell. Smell is a good emotional stimulus because the brain's olfactory system detects odours, quickly sends signals to the limbic system and links emotions with memories. We saw more shoppers coming into the baby aisle when the smell of Johnson's Baby Lotion was pumped into the air nearby. Similarly, one of the spirits companies experimented with the smell of juniper berries to encourage more shoppers to approach the gin fixture. Despite the success of some of these experiments, aside from the smell of the bakery that most supermarkets use, there has been little widespread use of smell to attract shoppers.

Signs that help the shopper to navigate the store – for example, bus-stop type signs that stick out from a fixture with a picture of the signpost brand – will increase the numbers of shoppers to that category. Once there, simple signs that help shoppers to choose can be influential. When these signs are appropriate to the emotional needs of the shopper, they can be very effective. This might be to highlight something that is new, or to offer reassurance about the choice. Reassurance can be provided in many ways; for example, with a simple endorsement highlighting that it is an "award winner", or an endorsement by a celebrity chef, or if it's pitched as 'the number one selling brand' in the category. A retailer we worked with in the US implemented a top-seller signage programme. Simple yellow labels were stuck to the shelf with the words "top-seller" in categories across the store. The varying levels of success of this approach reflected the nature of the different categories, but it was impressive. Some signs were successful in increasing sales by 10 – 15 per cent while others were game changing, increasing item sales by over 100 per cent. Overall, store sales grew by four per cent during the depths of recession.

As we move out of grocery stores into those retail channels where we are more prepared to invest time, we see many more conscious decisions being made. The more engagement we have with the product, the more involved our decision-making becomes.

Shopping in a typical High Street fashion store will take around ten minutes; if you buy something, you will probably spend another ten minutes. You are likely to fixate on about 80 products, giving each product around three fixations. You switch between general browse mode where the search is focused on reviewing products close to you, usually within two metres, and on colours, patterns and product details such as stitching, buttons or belts. This review and response process continues unconsciously as the shopper drifts. Once their attention is attracted by an emotional response to an item, the shopper will switch modes and begin touching the product. This sensory response appears to allow the shopper to imagine what the garment will both feel and look like to wear. The average shopper will do this "touch-picturing" about 15 times and if the garment is engaging, the shopper will pick up the product. Once this occurs, in addition to the emotional response produced by the product, the shopper will seek more rational information about issues such as price and sizing. This is the go/no-go moment.

Typically, 25 per cent of womenswear shoppers will use the changing room. This is a high intensity, stressful moment, not least because most of us are not used to removing our clothes in public. In this situation we make a very fast sequence of emotionally charged decisions, and this is reflected in the high number of arguments that originate here with couples shopping together. We trade off rational attributes such as cost against a predominantly emotional response to a garment. Here again, our emotional packets come into play; this time, alongside the perception of the retailer brand, memories with the garment's feel and style as well as our previous experience are also associated. Between 20 – 30 per cent of us will convert to make a purchase.

When we consider the choices we make and how we make them, it is important to understand that the emotional packet and rational factors come into play and compete as the purchase nears completion. The stronger the emotional packet is, the less influence that rational factors have on the final choice. For most shoppers, the store is an important component for the research and purchasing phases. Because some purchases, such as mobile phones, are made only very occasionally, shoppers in the researching phase use the store to categorise options and are much less likely to want to interact with staff. Once they are equipped with a better idea of their likely options, the shopper will then visit a store and discuss different options with staff to help finalize their choice.

A significant element of a brand's success is its visibility and emotional packet. And an important part of any brand's emotional packet is what its consumption actually delivers for us. This is explored in greater detail in the next chapter, which describes how shoppers make decisions and make choices for buying something that is unfamiliar.

9

Choosing and Using

"If it weren't for Philo T. Farnsworth, inventor of television, we'd still be eating frozen radio dinners."
Johnny Carson

Several vital aspects of shopping are often overlooked and deserve much greater focus. In particular, how do we choose to buy something that we aren't familiar with? What affects our decision-making? And what happens in the consumer's mind when they use or consume their purchase – just how significant is their experience of the product?

We have already seen that *learning* is the fundamental difference between decision-making for high interest and involvement products, such as mobile phones, and the marginal choice-making involved in most of our grocery shopping. Both types of decision-making involve the emotional packet, but to make sure I make the right mobile phone purchase I must make the effort to learn about the product and compare data. This matters, because it allows me to assess, somewhat rationally, the various product benefits and potential trade-offs.

The situation when I am buying other products is not always so clear. For example, imagine that I am buying from the category called recipe sauces; these are products that you add to a primary protein such as chicken to create a final meal. I have never used the category but I remember eating a meal made with one at a friend's house once. So when I approach the category I see that there are two large brand blocks: one is Dolmio, the other Ragu. Although I can't remember which brand my friend used, the visual language of the packaging and the large range within both of the brands suggests that they are major, mass-market brands. I then notice a third, much smaller brand: Loyd Grossman. Now, I'm somewhat at a disadvantage in that I don't watch television and I don't know who he is, yet the design of the packaging has colour and typeface that indicates a more upmarket brand. Do I use my phone and call a friend or should I call up the web to investigate the brand benefits? What would *you* do?

Conventional logic says that I make my choice by using the information presented by the brands. Sensible, but unrealistic; I actually make my choice using the shortcuts that the brands offer me. How large is each brand's block of products on the shelf? What are the packaging cues – is it mass appeal or upmarket? Where on the shelf are they located? These are the unconscious cues that I see and they lead me to make my decision. I may even use price to make a final choice.

So instead of making the effort to learn about the product and use that information to aid my decision-making, as I do with a mobile phone purchase, I prefer to use well-established cues to make personal assumptions that then lead me to my choice. These assumptions are likely, at best, to be erratic as they are not informed, but guesses.

This links to the final influence affecting the shopper's decision to buy the product again: the experience of using or consuming the product. In particular, does it match up to expectations? Does it deliver emotionally and rationally? For example, does the laundry detergent clean the clothes well enough? Does it match my expectations?

Changes in consumption affect the way that we shop and consumption in developed countries has changed significantly over the last 30 years. This is mainly because family structures have become less traditional and more diverse. In particular, we have a growing number of single-person households, ageing populations, and a greater number of adult households where both parents work. These changes result in greater pressures – notably in decreasing amounts of available time for managing the household. These social trends can also be seen in the markets that are developing fastest and currently emerging as the economic powerhouses of the 21st century, notably in Asia.

For example, according to Kantar Worldpanel, the research firm that conducts a survey of 24,000 households in the UK twice a year, the average food preparation time per day has dropped from 60 minutes in 1980 to just over 18 minutes in 2010. The average Briton spends more time watching cookery programmes than actually cooking, while cooking something from scratch accounts for only 25 per cent of evening meals in the UK.

It is a similar story in France, and especially in Paris – home to the world's best cooking and a mecca to seekers of "haute cuisine". It is also a country where 3,000 of its restaurants are closing every year, while McDonald's is opening 70 new outlets each year.

With many more people holidaying abroad, the same 30-year period has seena dramatic increase in foreign recipes as part of the UK diet. The same survey shows that while traditional British recipes still dominate, ethnic cuisines are growing quickly. Italian cuisine comprises around 20 per cent of meals, more than 10 per cent are Indian, and Chinese and Mexican are around five per cent each.

Despite these changes, as we have seen earlier, we are all still very conservative in the range of meals that we consume. The average consumer in the UK eats a repertoire of six and a half dishes in a two-week period.

Concerns about health and weight both appear to be behind food choices in developed markets, where increasing numbers of the population are clinically obese. According to recent OECD data, 30 per cent of Americans, 24 per cent of Mexicans, 23 per cent of British and 22 per cent of Slovakians are clinically obese. Over half of British shoppers are concerned with being overweight. Health and indulgence, however, are not mutually exclusive. Study the diet of most consumers and you will find that many people's day starts with an ambition to eat healthy products; by evening cravings, treats and indulgences appear. At the start of the week meals are healthy; as we reach the end of the week, indulgence again appears.

The pressure on traditional family structures, a feature of developed and some developing markets, has a dramatic effect on the importance of cooking and home care. These factors both have a discriminatory effect on store and brand choice. Talking to US cat owners recently, particularly those in female, single households, the percentage share of their own food budget is skewed: luxury packaged food for the cat at the expense of the quality of their own pre-packaged meals. In Asia, particularly in richer markets such as South Korea, Singapore and Japan, women are increasingly marrying later and in greater proportions than previously, not marrying at all. Today, in cities such as Tokyo, over 30 per cent of women aged 30 – 34 are single. This does not mean that they are cohabiting as they would in the West; instead, more and more women, particularly those that are educated, are choosing not to have a partner at all. This has several consequences: for instance, it affects how women shop (making frequent, small-basket shopping trips), and the fact that single men are either staying with their parents longer, or not food shopping at all but eating out instead. This reluctance to marry has also introduced the phenomenon of cross-border marriage. According to the book, *Asian Cross Border Marriage Migration*, by Melody Lu and Wen-Shan Yang, 27 per cent of Taiwanese marriages in 2002 involved foreign women. For retailers and brands, the implications include finding a sudden demand for new foods and recipes with the arrival of these brides. Demographic trends are profoundly affecting the way we shop as well as how and what we buy.

The role of brands varies, depending on where in the world you travel. Generally, international brands are the most trusted in the largest number of markets, notably Russia, where in a relatively short space of time they have gone from having no choice at all to an inrush of multinationals. Within a generation, Russian consumers have become hooked on international brands, displaying a level of trust that crushes opportunities for new, private label brands or existing Russian local brands. In India, among very low income families, brands are displayed but not used as a sign of affluence. I remember seeing a pack of OMO washing powder in a woman's kitchen; she still washed the family's clothing in the river, but the pack of precious washing powder, never used, was on display to her friends. In the UK, trust in retail brands is high. It is estimated that the private label market share will increase to 50 per cent of the total by 2025. Generally, the success of private label has a direct relationship with the level of trust in the host retailer. As a result, the brand positioning of the retailer is key for private label success.

This contrasts with the situation in some markets, particularly in Asia where generations of people have grown up in a culture of the group or community rather than that of the individual, and shoppers are much more likely to follow the lead of their community. A reliance on the wisdom of crowds means that if a crowd of people have started buying from a fixture, others will follow. There must be something good there! The legacy of former totalitarian countries is such that trust in information from normal sources (such as the government or church) was destroyed. People were far more likely to believe what their neighbours said in a food queue than information published by the authorities. In these countries, word of mouth among local trusted communities or communication by international brands are much more likely to be believed and acted upon.

Our consumption choices are often driven by a desire for self-expression. This is shown by a study of beer-buying habits in the Netherlands. Consumers in the east drink Grolsch, because this is where the brewery has been located since the 17th century. If you are invited to a party in the east and arrive with Heineken, are you trying to insult your host? Smokers will often smoke economy brands or roll their own cigarettes during the week, but come the weekend and the opportunity to socialize, the same consumers will smoke premium brands. Private label brands are often more successful in categories that are not on display. For example, washing powder is stored (and therefore hidden) in the cupboard under the sink – nobody is going to see you using it. Ketchup is used at the table and your children's friends can all see (and report) whether it is a branded or private label.

However successful a brand's pre-store development and in-store display, the product itself still has to deliver. This might mean delivering an emotional benefit, such as status. The purchase of a particularly sharp-looking coat is commented on by the opposite sex, for example, or the quality of the wine you serve is complemented by your dinner guests. Or it may be a more fundamental product delivery: the whites are noticeably whiter in the wash, my skin is notably smoother with the application of a particular moisturizer, or the food simply tastes great.

Most consumer societies evolve from needs to wants, to some degree following the theory developed by Dr Abraham Maslow. His theory, known as the hierarchy of needs, was first developed in the US in 1943 and published in his 1954 book, *Motivation and Personality*. While this approach was developed from an individualist American perspective, it is a useful tool for describing how consumers evolve from needs to wants. Maslow theorized that we start with *physiological* needs that keep us alive, such as breathing, food, water, sex and sleep. We then move to *safety* needs – security of body, family, property – and then on to *love or belonging* needs, such as friendship and family. The next, higher level of need is for *esteem*, reflected in confidence and the respect of others. The final stage is *self-actualisation*, which includes issues of morality, creativity and problem-solving, amongst many others. At the lower stages of this hierarchy of needs we require products that allow us to survive; as we move up the hierarchy we desire products that allow us to express ourselves either to others (status brands) or ourselves (membership brands, such as affiliation with a football club).

If we extend Maslow's thinking further, we can describe our ideas of self not just as a product of a social system such as Anglo-American, Chinese or Arab, but as something we actively express and create through our consumption. In a paper written in 1998, Richard Elliott of Oxford University describes how we all carry values that we have inherited, observed, partially considered or copied. We then express those values, our own self-narratives, through the products and brands that we consume. As a middle-class social conservative in the US, I would be much more likely to respond to certain brands, while as a liberal European I will choose other brands to express myself. If I am part of the new urban middle class in eastern China, I will again make different choices that express my self-image in the society where I live. We may flex those choices depending on our social contexts, but if what I am is made up of what I have and what I consume, then it is the symbolic meanings of brands and the emotions that we have vested in them that explains why emotions are such an important part of the emotional packet.

Taste is one of the traditional five senses and describes our ability to detect the flavours of food, minerals and, *in extremis*, poison. All basic tastes are described either as appetitive or aversive, depending on their effect on the body. These are sensed through the taste buds, small sensory organs concentrated on the upper surface of the tongue. The responses from these organs are brought to the brain via three cranial nerves: the front two-thirds of the tongue and soft palate have one route through the facial nerve, the vagus nerve is for the small taste area on the epiglottis, and a further nerve route is for the rear third of the tongue.

In addition to the basic tastes, our sensation of flavour is influenced by other factors such as smell, texture, temperature and spiciness. The basic tastes are sweetness, bitterness, sourness, saltiness and umami (a category of taste that corresponds to the flavour of glutamates, especially monosodium glutamate). Some researchers suggest that there is also a fatty substance taste receptor, as this has been detected in mice.

I recall being instructed in the basic art of tasting wine; I was told that it was vital to swirl the wine over all areas of the tongue, allowing the liquid to pass over the edge of each part and over the "taste belt". This was based on a common misconception about different sections around the edge of the tongue being exclusively responsible for different basic tastes. The misconception originated from a paper by Harvard psychologist Edwin G. Boring, who misinterpreted a translated German paper that was written in 1901. The paper actually suggested that there were minute differences in different areas of the tongue and whereas some parts of the tongue would be able to detect taste earlier, all parts of the tongue would be equally good at assessing the different tastes.

Sweetness, usually regarded a pleasurable sensation, is mainly the result of the presence of sugars and depends on the activation of at least two types of sweetness receptors. Bitterness is the most sensitive of the basic tastes, perhaps partly because a large number of bitter compounds are toxic, and it is sensed in products such beer, coffee and olives. Sourness denotes acidity, often present in fruit such as lemons and grapes. Saltiness is a response to the presence of sodium ions (such as salt) in food, or ions from alkali metals such as calcium. Umami is a relatively new discovery. The word itself is borrowed from the Japanese and its quality is described as savoury or meaty. Products such as cheese, soy sauce and anything with monosodium glutamate have a strong umami taste. Umami taste is fundamental to most Eastern cuisines.

There are other sensations that the tongue can feel, largely as a result of detection by the somatosensory system. These include: calcium; coolness, including a minty taste; dryness, such as the tannin taste of red wine or rhubarb; numbness, including the tingling sensation produced by spices such as Sichuan pepper; heartiness or kokumi present in alcohol-laden foods; and spiciness, a sensation of hotness created by ingredients such as chilli and black pepper. The final sensation is temperature, felt in a chilled beer or a hot soup.

The tastes or sensory experiences we enjoy when consuming products become memories, alongside other memories we have of that particular brand, and these are all added to the emotional packet. Crucially, the consumption phase does not only include the sensory experience of consuming, such as eating or wearing, but also the ergonomic experience of *using*. Our brains are designed to respond positively to things that make our motor actions easier. Given two packages of the same product and brand, if one is designed to be easier to pick up, we are more likely to choose that pack. I was laughed at for carrying both the laptop provided by TNS, my business, and my Apple Macbook while writing this book. The ergonomic design of the Macbook meant that writing was easier and I was happy to carry two laptops through countless airports just for the sensory reward of having the Macbook.

Another factor influencing usage at home is visibility. The average UK household has 42 fridge openings, 24 cupboard openings and eight freezer openings within a week. This means that how we store products in terms of their visibility in the cupboard or freezer, as well as the frequency that we use that location, will influence whether the product is seen and the extent to which it is used. The packaging designer needs not only to consider the "shopper face", the visual cues that the shopper uses to recognize the brand on the shelf, but also the product's "consumer face". Depending on how the product is packed onto the shelf of the cupboard will also determine whether it stimulates usage. For example, Coca-Cola's fridge packs not only determine a good location in the fridge. The packaging is also designed to be visible on the fridge shelf and therefore increase opportunities for impulse consumption.

If we have the product's consumption delivery organized and we understand the dynamics of presentation in-store, there is the other major influence on the development of the emotional packet: pre-store marketing. How products are marketed (or not) using the emotional packet – and, in particular, how we create appeal – is the focus of the next chapter.

10 | Creating Appeal and Establishing Memories

*"Advertising may be described as the science of arresting human
intelligence long enough to get money from it."*
Stephen Leacock

Early in 2009, I was invited to speak at a conference in Cracow,
Poland's second largest city and a leading centre of Polish
academic, cultural and artistic life. The event was one of the first
conferences focusing on *neuromarketing* – a rather ugly way of
describing the use of neuroscience to understand the impact of
marketing. This field includes respectable neuroscientists but it
also contains its share of less reputable ones who assert all sorts
of quackery (a fact highlighted in a recent issue of the *Harvard
Review of Psychiatry*).

The conference was organized by an energetic and passionate
expert, should be Rafal Ohme, now owner of one of the most
successful neuromarketing agencies in the world and at that
time, a professor at the Warsaw School of Social Psychology
and the Polish Academy of Sciences. Also speaking was Tim
Ambler who has written some of the subject's most influential
academic papers of the early 21st century. He focuses on using
neuroscience to investigate potential new ways of thinking
about the effect of advertising. Later at the same conference I
was also fortunate to meet another influential and feisty cage-

rattler, Robert Heath, whose work was mentioned previously. The importance of their work in advertising connects strongly with what we have learnt about how shoppers shop.

In earlier chapters we have seen how decision-making behaviour is rarely conscious, ordered or rational, particularly in the world of grocery retailing. In fact, the advertising world's reliance on what is known as *hierarchy of effects* models, which assume the contrary, has been both the most damaging and possibly the most significant influence on advertising in the 20th century. The hierarchy of effects model is a term that, very broadly speaking, covers a sequence of five steps that a consumer follows from their initial exposure to a product or advertisement to their decision to buy. These five steps are: awareness, interest, evaluation, conviction and purchase. Other models have been suggested, for example: *classical cognitive models* that follow the idea that we think, then do, then feel; *non-cognitive models* which propose that there is no thinking; *elaboration likelihood models* proposing that we like to assume a "correct" attitude that motivates us to pay attention, but even if we are not motivated we will still see peripheral cues; a *scanning focusing model* and *heuristic systematic model of persuasion* that assess different kinds of involvement; and *integrative models* that combine involvement with emotional response.

Much of the advertising industry's thinking has assumed that consumers were rationally trading off different product benefits against cost and calculating, rationally, to achieve the best value. As we have seen in the low involvement categories of the grocery world and in the higher involvement world of fashion and phones, for example, decision-making can best be described as "low-energy, marginal choice making". People have been assuming a level of rigour, objectivity and understanding in the minds of consumers that is simply not there. Most of the time, when we buy we are making assumptions about brands by using information that is emotionally-based and has been gathered unreliably. This is particularly the case when a purchasing decision has a relatively small impact on our lives; for example, buying the wrong brand of washing-up liquid is unlikely to disrupt most people's lives too much. Consequently, the erratically-gathered information in our emotional packets is rarely subjected to a rational analysis. Instead, we prefer to use the shortcut of a "brand" to provide a summary; a probable version of a product that is broadly acceptable to our needs from the category.

One of the most popular advertising models is attention-interest-desire-action (AIDA) which assumes a linear, rational sequence of decisions that simply does not occur in reality. Not only does the model ignore any pre-existing awareness in consumers, the simplistic metaphor of cause and effect also fails to account for the multitude of inputs that form the emotional packet.

Valuable research and analysis of the effects of advertising is provided by Spike Cramphorn from an advertising research company called add+impact. This research utilises the new thinking about emotional decision-making and the role of the unconscious. Crucially, it helps to describe how advertising actually works as well as undermining traditional beliefs in linear models.

The researchers used data accumulated from the responses of around a quarter of a million people to 4,000 advertisements in 40 different countries across the main media types: television, radio, etc. They then grouped respondents' opinions about these ads into three groups:

Advertising Attention – where there were strong feelings in response to the ad, either positive or negative.

Brand Feeling – which highlighted how the ad made each person feel – for example, "this is a brand that people like me use".

Brand News – where something new about the brand was communicated.

The researchers then looked at the connection between these statements and the respondents' purchasing intentions: whether or not they were consistent with their claimed intentions to buy the brand. Whilst this rationalized opinion is unlikely to play out in the real world it does at least provide a comparable measure of intention.

163

Of the three factors, brand feeling was the measure that linked to an intention to purchase, but there was no flow between the earlier stages. Nothing in the AIDA model explains the origins of the brand feeling. Inspired by some of Tim Ambler's work which proposed that consumers do not start with a clean sheet of information about a brand or category, they introduced a fourth factor: that of *brand experience*. (In fact, Tim Ambler suggested a different approach to AIDA, proposing instead that brand experience would be influenced by memory, affect (the "brand feeling") and conation or thinking. This approach is known as the MAC model. The stronger the positive memory, the more likely the consumer is to buy the brand. This approach is more in line with contemporary thinking – that we feel, then do, then think, rather than the historical idea that we think, do and then feel.

After analysing the fourth factor of brand experience it was seen as having a positive impact on all of the MAC factors (memory, affect and conation or thinking). *Memory* of the brand certainly affects purchasing intentions but not as strongly as brand feeling. *Affect* (or brand feeling) and *conation* are triggered by brand experience and these also have an effect on purchasing intentions.

Too often, the relationship between the unconscious and advertising has been ignored. The Orwellian, mid-20th century concept of "subliminal advertising" helped to create this irrational fear, which is contradicted by science. In fact, understanding and managing the stimuli that affect the brain and produce mental reactions is simply an extension of existing best practices. In addition, the term "subliminal advertising" was itself coined as a result of a falsified experiment by James Vicaray, pandering to the hysteria of a bygone age.

In 1957 James Vicaray claimed that in an experiment where moviegoers were repeatedly shown a 0.03 second advert for Coca-Cola and popcorn, sales of these products substantially increased. Bearing in mind that this occurred just a few years after the McCarthy hearings and at a time when Cold War fears were firmly taking root, suggestions of mind infiltration not only induced wide publicity but also resulted in a report by the CIA that led to so-called "subliminal advertising' being banned. Some suggest that the original research was never carried out – certainly some years later James Vicaray admitted that the study was a gimmick and that the amount of data was too small to be meaningful. The legacy, however, lives on in urban myth.

Robert Heath's research, inspired by Herbert Krugman in the early seventies, suggests that when we watch television advertising, our attention is not necessarily required for the advert to have an effect. When an advert interrupts a movie, sport or sitcom that we are watching, very few of us gasp with excitement and lean forward to watch intently. Voluntary attention, where we continuously return our attention to its object whenever it wanders away, is present when we are thinking, learning or reading. We are much less likely to put in this effort when viewing changing stimuli such as films and television and especially when watching advertising. Most people partially disconnect the brain's visual feed, thinking instead about non-related subjects. This response is the same as we saw with the shopper in the queue or attached to the fuel pump in the forecourt. They may be looking around them but they are not really seeing. As we previously discussed, Robert Heath suggests that the brain works in two states: high, conscious attention and low-level, unconscious response to the environment. This is something that we've seen already when studying the shopper.

For example, imagine I ask you to watch an advert and afterwards I ask you some questions about what you recall – a typical advertising research scenario. This fails to create the "lean back comfort" you experience at home and is therefore questionable for its value. Usually, having given the advert more attention than you would normally, you would probably be able to describe certain scenes. These memories result from high, conscious attention and may well be some of the things that you might recall about the advertising in an interview some weeks later. However, at the same time we are also unconsciously processing information about the advert using low attention, and there are aspects you would be unable to recall. This is part of the same process of memory formation and unconscious learning of colours and shapes that happens when you are in a store and is so important for recognizing familiar brands as we previously described in the Gillette advertising.

While attention to an advert generally contributes to a theoretical intention to purchase, all the work that we have done in-store suggests that low attention processing related to advertising is probably much more important than the advertising industry has ever realized. The main role of brand experience actually appears to be that it acts as a stimulant. It is no surprise that existing brand users are likely to feel more positive about the brand, but there is no sequencing between the factors. According to the research, we find that it is primarily brand feeling that contributes most to an intention to purchase, and a small amount of that from giving attention to the ad, a small amount for interest in news and a small amount from existing habit.

Spike Cramphorn's "brand feeling" is, therefore, very significant, and its effects are not short-term. Instead, brand feeling is the collation of experiences and the long-term relationship between a brand and a person, and the emotional packet that we discussed earlier. Another excellent book, *The Advertised Mind,* by Erik du Plessis, concludes by introducing another term, the "brand soma", again inspired by Damasio's somatic marker hypothesis. Du Plessis argues that the soma is a simple limbic reaction, a response from the instinctive, emotional part of the brain. This response may be as simple as "liking" or "disliking" and is then processed as a much more complex emotion. The emotional filter also helps to decide whether a memory is laid down and if so, the strength of that memory. This is how the emotional packet builds and strengthens with advertising as one of many influencers on it.

In addition, Robert Heath and Paul Feldwick, in a more recent paper, discuss the idea that visuals, sounds, symbols, music, gestures, context and so on are not necessarily an aid to recall or a means of attracting attention. Instead, they are themselves communicators and in turn, influence the emotional packet. For example, the short music clip that is played whenever the Intel chip is featured in advertising contributes to our feeling and experience of the brand. This does more than simply attract our attention since the sequence is usually played after the end of another advertisement for computers.

The fact that Coca-Cola is a great marketing business is broadly true. However, for many people the strong emotional packet that created the results that we saw earlier from the Pepsi Challenge is not just achieved through great advertising or even great in-store activity, although no doubt these are important. Instead, Coke's powerful brand results from the emotional strength of the memories that are formed when, as children, a Coke is a much anticipated treat. The strong, positive memories of a Coke that are laid down in childhood (including excitement, taste experience and anticipation) altogether provide a powerful bedrock for the formal marketing activity that filters into the emotional packet later.

Certainly, popular advertising may strengthen the emotional packet, as with any positive experience of a brand, but these are relatively minor in their overall significance. The job of the marketer is to attempt to manage the emotional packet positively, while accepting that there are many other uncontrollable aspects that also contribute to the packet – such as seeing other people consume the brand.

A good example is provided by newspapers. Most British people, on seeing someone buy a copy of the *Financial Times*, would make a series of judgments about the likely lifestyle, politics and attitudes of the purchaser, just as there would be a different series of assumptions attached to purchasers of *The Guardian* or a tabloid newspaper. This is the expression of our emotional packets. So for some people, the brand values of *The Guardian* fit best with their self-image and their emotional packet is most closely aligned with *that* brand. This operates in many markets. *The New York Times* has a definable brand position that differs to that of *The Wall Street Journal* in the US, *Le Monde* versus *Le Figaro* in France, etc.

The findings of the research support the idea that advertising's role is not to move a consumer along a linear, hierarchical model. Instead, it is to build the stock of a brand's emotional packet. If further evidence were needed, remember that we know that consumers who already use a brand are unsurprisingly, much more likely to consume advertising activity for that brand.

This brief journey to consider advertising has two purposes. First, that even the most heavily invested-in aspect of marketing has significant flaws, and second, that without connecting to the journey of the shopper, all that preliminary work is potentially wasted.

Once we move into the store, it is the emotional packet that matters, and this is triggered by the brand's colourshape as well as good shelf positioning offering strong visibility. The emotional packet is often well-established before the shopper arrives, and it is this that determines the success or failure of all that expenditure designed to influence the customer. The emotional packet is not just developed by advertising; there are many less formal ways that we learn about brands and the store is one of the key locations for this.

In situations where we make low-energy, marginal choices, the connection between brand exposures both before and at the fixture are fundamental. The industry has to refocus its attention and expenditure onto understanding how the available and habitual shoppers make their marginal choices and develop brand feeling and visibility strategies – both before arriving at the store and at the fixture – to persuade these shoppers.

The final chapter looks at the future of shopping: the issues that will affect shoppers' behaviour, the competitive, persuasive techniques that retailers and brands are developing, and the future for shopper research. Like the act of shopping itself, this is an activity and business that continues to develop and change.

11

Where Next?

"The future is nothing but a gathering of the consequences of the past, but the past – which one day will also enfold us – is the creation of our echo."
Donald MacLaren, Chief of the
MacLarens, in conversation

When the study of shoppers and shopping was first pioneered some 25 years ago, we were trying to talk to brands and retailers that had not really considered the subject. Most of us started by adapting consumer research techniques and then moved on to create new specialist methods, before pushing into new territories of observation and ethnography. More recently, we are at the forefront of the adoption of psycho-physiological and neuroscientific research, working with some of the leading academics and universities in the field.

Most of the small, ground-breaking agencies that developed the study of shoppers and shopping have now been acquired by the largest, global research agencies. These firms now have shopper research as a core part of the global service offer, and most brands and retailers consider it an important part of their learning programmes. One of the challenges for our clients has been to adapt and implement these new insights into their existing business processes – perhaps inevitably this can be a slow and difficult process. This means that we not only have to be excellent at producing great insights, but we also have to help brands and retailers realize the opportunities that these insights offer.

In trying to launch the idea of shopper research into an industry where the outcomes sometimes challenged their fundamental ways of doing business, shopper insight has often fallen into the trap of becoming isolated: a standalone silo within the larger organization. This is the immediate challenge that brands and retailers are currently exploring. As a result, much of the pioneering work being done today is not focused on developing new research techniques. Instead, it is about testing new ways to make information about shoppers flow into these established business practices. The most enlightened businesses, particularly some of the multinational brands, are turning their attention to connecting what they already know about consumers to this new shopper knowledge.

If we consider some of the big breakthroughs of the past that were based on consumer insights, it is now evident that a stronger connection to shoppers would have either made those innovations more successful, or have contributed to them avoiding failure.

In the 1990s, Birds Eye Walls, a frozen foods business, recognized from their research into consumers' habits that there was an emerging trend favouring pre-prepared meals. Birds Eye Walls put significant investment into developing a large range of products that would allow consumers to create fantastic meals from freezer to table in a quick and convenient manner. That investment included a large amount of money put into product development, advertising, packaging and product launch, and they received positive consumer feedback. Yet despite their research and follow-up work, it failed.

Quite simply, the firm failed because of a lack of understanding of the frozen food shopper. Most of their potential target market either didn't shop for frozen food at all, or at best, whizzed into the area to collect frozen vegetables and ice cream, ignoring the rest of the area. Consequently, all their appealing products remained hidden away in freezers, unvisited and unseen, and all their investment was lost.

Consider beer, often a category in long-term decline in the face of competition from wine. Research insights revealed that consumers were no longer happy to drink bitter that tasted of tins and didn't at all resemble the product they could happily enjoy in pubs. So, some clever technological development went into widgets that would create the same taste that was found in pubs and bars. Despite huge investment and massive advertising the products were almost invisible and only managed to limp through their appearance in-store, largely through word of mouth. Luckily, enough consumers found the product and told enough of their friends about it to make it into a success.

Another interesting example is provided by Pringles, the brand that reinvented the crisps and snacks category. This was formerly the territory of products and brands that were single pack accompaniments to meals. This time, Procter Gamble invested in research into how shoppers shopped the category. As a result, they created a stand-out fixture that allowed the packaging, developed around the idea of sharing and what was called a "big night in", to be visible. Tubes that were displayed on special shelves had strong visibility in an aisle full of traditional crisp bags and supported by strong advertising, the product was a success.

The future will be a world where brands and retailers consider shoppers in their strategic plans in a way that is routine, comprehensive and not by chance. It will be a world where the decision-making happening at the shelf drives nearly all the development work that happens with categories and brands. In addition to the choices made at the shelf, other, vital activities will also inform the way that brands and retailers operate. In particular, they will consider the level of habituation, depth of commitment to brands at the fixture, the established search and selection processes for habitual and available shoppers, shopping styles at the fixture, established behavioural scripts, signpost brand responses and use of cognitive maps and, perhaps most importantly, the *colourshapes* of brands. All of these issues will feature in marketing activities, ranging from the initial concept for new products through to their packaging and display in-store.

Brands and retailers will think about the experiential aspect not only of the consumption of the product, but also about its selection in-store. It is unlikely that many categories will return to having a sales person in the store, and brands will have to think much harder about how to improve the effectiveness of the marketing they do before the shopper even reaches the store, and connect this with product sitting on the "warehouse" shelf. Instead of packaging being just boxes or cans, the Apple approach to packaging, making the sensory appeal of the packaging part of the product itself, will increase performance at shelf. How the product feels in the hand reflects the brand itself.

This work will have a major effect on how the retailing and marketing industry is structured and operates, with added impact on how money can be made. This will be similar to the disrupting effect that the internet and surrounding technologies have challenged other industries to consider, and as a result, change their strategies. For instance, consider the music industry, where the means of production, marketing and distribution have changed completely in a generation.

With the long term economic downturn, in several advanced retailing markets we are seeing the final death throes of once-mighty beasts, as retailers and brands both leap into the murky pool of promotions, each brand and retailer vying with the other to win the battle through ever-deeper promotions, whilst all the time steadily losing the war. "Buy one get one free" is morphing into "buy one get two free". As discussed earlier, we are training shoppers not to buy brands, most of which are broadly the same anyway, but to buy from a portfolio of similar products dependent on which one is on promotion this week. There is no way back from here. Once shoppers get used to this, the industry cannot turn around and try to sell everything at full price again.

The outcome is likely to be that brands will have to combine the full force of their understanding of consumers and shoppers together with all the various techniques of pre-store and in-store marketing, and focus on developing fewer, new products and line extensions. They will do this so that they are better able to develop brands that are truly differentiated in terms of their values, presence in-store and delivery. Brands that can manage the trick of combining a sense of provenance and locality, environmental credentials and honesty will be the megabrands of tomorrow. Otherwise, brands will become meaningless commodities sold at barely profitable margins; and particularly as more shopping moves online, price as a differentiator disappears.

As our homes become smarter the technology in our lives will take over the shopping for low-interest categories. The fridge will identify that milk is running low, or that we need to replenish our normal choice of yoghurts. The cupboard under the sink will know that the washing-up liquid is running out and the shower will inform us that we need more shampoo. Why would we need to order via supermarket.com? This monitoring technology will function as part of an online buying group that automatically negotiates a price with source suppliers and distributes via established home delivery networks. It cuts out the retailer altogether and makes price choices redundant – since it is always the lowest.

This scenario challenges retailers, who are currently merging their online and offline businesses to create reasons why shoppers would want to travel to their stores. Retailers currently play a valuable role in sifting through the choices presented by the buyer. In the future, this value-adding role becomes pivotal. The retailer will not simply be the price negotiator, they will also encourage shoppers to visit the store by identifying brands that are truly different and beneficial, and bring exclusive new product developments to the store. Whatever happens, we will move away from a warehouse of metal shelves to a space that focusses on using technology to increase the efficiency of shopping in low interest categories and bring entertainment to higher interest categories.

Retailers in Germany and Switzerland are experimenting with RFID to remove the need for unpacking and repacking purchases at the checkout. In the normal supply chain, each branded product has an identifying code, the bar code. With RFID, each individual product of each branded product has a unique code on a radio frequency tag. This enables adapted trolleys to scan the product into the trolley when the shopper puts it in, turning the trolley into a checkout. Also, as smartphones become more widespread we will see brands sending offers to the shopper's phone as they approach the relevant category. When the data from the loyalty card migrates onto our phones, retailers will know the brand that each shopper normally buys. Consequently, each shopper will potentially receive a customized offer sent directly from the brand to their phone as they approach the fixture, no matter which retailer they are in.

There is undoubtedly a social aspect to shopping. For some social groups it is their only chance to escape from home, whether this is due to relative poverty or other social conditions, such as caring for relatives. Some retailers in developed markets are perhaps considering these social issues as they expand from mass merchandising into financial services, and as they experiment with not only building the store but also the surrounding town, by selling the houses, the mortgages and perhaps the support infrastructure as well.

The internet and mobile communication was predicted to create a world of obese, couch-bound screen addicts. Instead, social networking has created new means of drawing people together, whether in protest, celebration or new communities, both online and offline. We are only a few short years away from complete experiential entertainment where, instead of being trapped on sofas and locked into televisions, we will be going onstage to sing a song, virtually living in a celebrity house, feeling the thrill of driving a rally car, potentially feeling some of the pain of getting in a ring, or re-fighting the Battle of Arnhem, all in our own homes. With this ever-increasing sensory overload, the places that we choose to visit in the bricks and mortar world will have to do much, much more than hang a dress on a hanger or plonk a jar of mayonnaise on a shelf to attract us. Consumer to consumer reviews and "If you like that, you'll like this" are the start of using technology to improve service and sales.

We are now moving into a period of long-term decline in the West, with its values falling under the under the influence of new influence of economic empires with different cultural norms. The individualism of the cowboy is challenged by the inclusiveness and localism of countries like China, Russia and India. This doesn't mean that one will replace the other; instead of Scooby-Doo my grandchildren will perhaps be consuming some version of entertainment that combines and grows these cultural values in a new way. The declining importance of privacy in our lives as we trade access to communication, information or entertainment for reduced levels of personal secrecy, accords with this cultural trend. We have, perhaps, reached the zenith of a desire for choice and individuality, and are now swinging back towards a world where all of our lives and thoughts are shared in real time. Perhaps making all of these choices, all of the time, is too difficult, and a world of homogeneity is more appealing. Indeed as Susan Greenfield suggests in her book, *Tomorrow's People*, as we broadcast and record all of our thoughts and behaviours, do we even need to use our memories anymore?

This prompts the question: how will brands intervene and become part of that collectivization? Do they use innovation to become the new generics (the Hoover of the vacuuming world), or do they curtail investment in individual brand marketing and simply supply retailers and their private brands?

In the future, new retailing opportunities will be created, both in terms of where we retail and how we do so. These opportunities are being driven largely by demographic changes and especially ageing populations around the world, not just in the established markets of Japan and Italy but also in China, combined with working populations that will not see retirement until their mid-seventies. In this situation, some retailers will choose to focus on a time and cash-rich population that will demand greater integration with their community and place much higher demands on service, potentially extending healthcare into the home as part of a social service. Other businesses may see an opportunity to bring retail directly to the places where people work, highlighted by Tesco's recent launch of real size posters of products on shelves in the Seoul subway. With this initiative, shoppers can select products using their smartphones while waiting for the train home, where their products will be delivered later.

Food technology, and in particular nanotechnology, will allow us to indulge our extravagant tastes whilst actually eating healthy products.

Something that tastes and feels like ice cream can be re-engineered at an atomic or molecular level so that it has no more fat than a cucumber, or a burger can be re-engineered to actually lower cholesterol. A margarine brand like Flora currently markets itself as doing exactly that: it has the potential to extend its brand value into new categories, so that perceived health benefits are given greatest prominence.

Other brands are considering buying back their shares from the stock market so they can create new business models that are focused not on value creation for shareholders, but value creation for charities and non-governmental organizations. This leads to a situation where, potentially, when we buy a bottle of spring water in an affluent part of the world we are funding the development of a well in an arid part of the world. In the same situation, retailers may see it as a commercial opportunity to engage with low income/low health communities and re-educate shoppers and consumers through food demonstrations, tastings and social gatherings in their stores. Those stores will no longer be full of warehoused products because it will all be delivered to our homes from the real warehouses. Enlightened perhaps? But if the average life expectancy of a man in areas of Glasgow's East End in Scotland is 51 years, compared with the UK average of around 80, keeping him alive for a further 30 years will also keep him buying for a further 30.

It has been a fascinating journey of discovery, watching and learning about how humans behave around the world, doing what might be considered the most mundane of tasks. This study of trading and exchange reveals some of the most fundamental characteristics of humanity. It is, perhaps, heartening to consider that when I am asked to describe what I have done for a living, almost everyone I talk to opens their response with: "Well, you would hate to watch me. I don't behave anything like a normal shopper." Well, I wouldn't, because so much of how we behave, regardless of origin, location or culture, is shared.

Thanks

A few years ago I went to the Speech Day at my children's school. An invited speaker, an ex pupil who was now a broadcaster, was invited to talk to us. He asked an audience of around 400 parents who, at the age of 14, had known what career they wanted to pursue? Around half the audience put up their hands. And then he asked for the same show of hands for anyone who was actually pursuing that career. Three out of the whole audience.

Like many involved in retailing, I fell into the area – my dreams were of being a musician and an artist which I am finally, rather late in life, returning to. This book tells part of the story of how I went from the shop floor to setting up my own business and, after a combination of hard work and luck, came to helping roll out the methods we had invented to a global practice at TNS, the company who purchased my agency.

There have been many, many people who have also worked very hard to contribute towards my luck over the past twenty years and I've loved working with them. Some of the many great people over the years at Magasin were Andrew Freer, Rob Lawson, Mark and Bridget Shrive, Lawrence Golding, Tina Ransom, Jeff and Claire Williams, Marjorie Epson, Tony Wren, Paul Ransom, Ali Alden, Paula Stimpson, Cheryl Gibson, Glenis Sawford,

Kevin "bloody" Wilkinson, Kathy Thompson, Bromley boys, Claire Noyon, Piers Tanner and Emilie Burrows. Thank you and all the many others at Magasin for your years of help and friendship.

Being bought out by a PLC that is the 2nd largest research agency in the world could have been very painful but there have been some great people in the global team who have made that transition fascinating. Thanks particularly to Barry Lemmon, Dan Boehm, Herb (the preacher) Sorensen, James Sorensen, Pat McCann and Susan Thomas. We've had some fun riding the wave!

Most of all, we wouldn't exist without the clients that in the early days took the risk, and in later years, promoted us as an agency, often in the teeth of entrenched opposition to new thinking. Some names of many are Chris Cole, Jeff Goode, Graham Jenkins, Chris Poole, Sarah Lacey, Neil Munro, Chris Connor, Joe Ward, Michael Dargan, John Bridge, Martin Southgate, Lindsey Hills and Martin Templar. Often, in addition to using us as an agency these and many others pushed us further along our journey of exploration.

Finally, many thanks to Jeremy Kourdi who made my scribbles readable and to Neil Munro, Cristina de Balanzo Bono, Christine Kane and Karin Peterson who took the time out of incredibly busy lives to read, comment and improve on the book. I have used many research papers in the process of developing the thinking outlined in the book and have included a bibliography – whilst these great scientists might not agree with my interpretation of their work, I hope I have done justice to their important contributions to science.

Bibliography

AMBLER, T. "Persuasion, pride and prejudice: how ads work". *International Journal of Advertising.* Vol. 19 (2000), No. 3, p. 299-315.

AMBLER, T. [et al.] "Salience and choice: Neural correlates of shopping decisions". *Psychology and marketing.* Vol. 21 (2004), No. 4, p.247-261.

AMBLER, T.; BURNE, T. "The impact of affect on memory of advertising". *Journal of Advertising Research.* Vol. 39 (1999), No. 2, p. 25-34.

AMBLER, T.; IOANNIDES, A.; ROSE, S. "Brands on the brain: neuro-images of advertising". *Business strategy review.* Vol. 11 (2000), No. 3, p. 17.

ASTOLFI, L. [et al.]. "Assessing the memorization of TV commercials with the use of high resolution EEG: a pilot study". *Conference Proceedings: Annual international Conference of the IEEE Engineering in Medicine and Biology Society. IEEE Engineering in Medicine and Biology Society. Conference,* 2008. Vol. 2008, p. 3755-3758.

ASTOLFI, L. [et al.]. "Neural basis for brain responses to TV commercials: a high-resolution EEG study". *IEEE transactions on neural systems and rehabilitation engineering: a publication of the IEEE Engineering in Medicine and Biology Society.* Vol. 16 (2008), No. 6, p. 522-531.

ASTOLFI, L. [et al.]. "The track of brain activity during the observation of TV commercials with the high-resolution EEG technology".

Computational intelligence and neuroscience. (2009), p. 652078-652078.

AWH, E; ARMSTRONG, K.M.; MOORE, T. "Visual and oculomotor selection: Links causes and implications for spatial attention" *Trends in cognitive sciences.* Vol. 10 (2006), No. 3, p.124-130.

BLANCHETTE, I.; RICHARDS, A. "The influence of affect on higher level cognition: a review of research on interpretation, judgement, decision making and reasoning". *Cognition & Emotion,* Psychology Press. (21 August 2009), p. 1-74

BRAUN-LATOUR, K.; LATOUR, M. "Assessing the long-term impact of a consistent advertising campaign on consumer memory". *Journal of Advertising.* Vol. 33 (2004), No. 2, p. 49.

BREWER, J.B. [et al.] "Making memories: brain activity that predicts how well visual experience will be remembered". *Science (New York, N.Y.).* Vol. 281 (1998), No. 5380, p. 1185-1187.

CACIOPPO, J.T.; PETTY, R.E. "Effects of message repetition and position on cognitive response, recall and persuasion". *Journal of Personality and Social Psychology.* Vol. 27 (1979), p. 97-109.

CHAIKEN, S. "Heuristic versus systematic information processing and the use of source versus message cues in persuasion". *Journal of Personality and Social Psychology.* Vol. 39 (1980), No. 5, p. 752-766.

CHANDON, P. [et al.] "Does in-store marketing work? Effects of the number and position of shelf facings on brand attention and evaluation at the point of purchase". *Journal of Marketing.* Vol. 73 (2009), p.1-17.

CRAMPHORN, S. "How to use advertising to build brands". *International Journal of Market Research.* 48.3 (2006): 255–276.

DE BALANZO BONO, C., SERRANO ABAD, N. "Fundamentals for the construction of an advertising communication model from the neuroscience perspective" International Communication Conference Malaga University (Spain) 2010.

FALLANI, F.D.V. [et al.]. "Structure of the cortical networks during successful memory encoding in TV commercials". *Clinical Neurophysiology.* Vol. 119 (2008), p. 2231-2237.

FISHER, C.E.; CHIN, L; KLITZMAN, R. "Defining neuromarketing: practices and profesional challenges" *Harvard Review of Psychiatry.* Vol 18 (2010), No. 4, p.230-237.

GILL, R.S. "An eye-tracking study investigating the effects of in-store marketing on brand salience". MBA Thesis 2011, University of Leicester.

GOTTLEIB, J "From thought to action: The Parietal Cortex as a bridge between Perception, Action and Cognition" *Neuron Review.* Vol. 53 (2007), p. 9-16.

GREENFIELD, S. *Tomorrow's People: How 21st Century technology is changing the way we think and feel.* Penguin, 2003.

HEATH, R. "Low involvement processing: a new model of brands and advertising". *International Journal of Advertising.* Vol. 19 (2000), No. 3, p. 287-298.

HEATH, R.; FELDWICK, P "50 years using the wrong model of advertising" *International Journal of Market Research.* Vol. 50 Issue 1, p. 29-59.

HUANG, R.S.; DAWES, J. "Price promotions: How much volume is discounted that would sell anyway at the normal price?" Report 43 for Corporate Members (December 2007), Ehrenberg-Bass Institute for Marketing Science.

KNUTSON, B. [et al.]. «Neural predictors of purchases». *Neuron.* Vol. 53 (2007), No. 1, p. 147-156.

KRAULIS, R.J. "The control of voluntary eye movements: New Perspectives". *The Neuroscientist.* Vol. 11 (2005) p. 124-137.

KRUGMAN, H.E. "The impact of television advertising: learning without involvement". *Public Opinion Quarterly.* Vol. 29 (1965), No. 3, p. 349-356.

KRUGMAN, H.E. "Brain wave measures of media involvement". *Journal of Advertising Research.* Vol. 11 (1971), p. 3-9.

KRUGMAN, H.E. "Memory without recall, exposure without perception". *Journal of Advertising Research.* Vol. 17 (1977), p. 3-10.

LAMME, V.A.F.; ROELFSEMA, P.R. "The distinct modes of vision offered by feedforward and recurrent processing". *Trends in Neurosciences.* Vol. 23 (2000), No. 66, p. 530-558.

LANG, A. "Involuntary attention ad psycho physiological arousal evoked by structural features and mild emotions in TV commercials". *Communication Research.* Vol. 17 (1990), No. 3, p. 275-299.

MILLER, M.B.; GAZZANIGA, M.S. "Creating false memories for visual scenes". Neuropsychologia Vol.36 (1998), No. 6, p.513-520.

MOORE, T, ARMSTRONG, K.M., FALLAH, F "Visuomotor origins of covert spatial attention" *Neuron.* Vol. 40 (2003), p. 671-683.

MORRIS, J.D. [et al.]. «The power of affect: predicting intention». *Journal of Advertising Research.* Vol. 42 (2002), No. 3, p. 7-17.

MCCLURE, S. [et al.] "Neural correlates of behavioural preference for culturally familiar drinks" *Neuron.* Vol. 44 (2004) p. 379-387.

NORMAN, H.; ROMANIUK, J.; RIEBE, E. "100 per cent brand loyals exposed". Report 35 for Corporate Members (2005), Ehrenberg-Bass Institute for Marketing Science.

OHME, R.; REYKOWSKA, D.; WIENER, C.A. (In press). "Application of frontal EEG asymmetry to advertising research: Sony Bravia case". *Journal of economical psychology.* Special edition: Decision in neuroscience.

RAYNER, K. "Eye Movements in Reading and Information Processing: 20 years of research". *Psychological Bulletin.* Vol, 124 (1998), No. 3, p. 372-422.

ROEDIGER, H.L.III, MCDERMOTT, K.B. "Creating False Memories: Re-membering words not presented in lists". *Journal of Experimental Psychology: Learning, memory and cognition* Vol.21 (1995), No. 4 p. 803-814.

ROMANIUK, J; SHARP, B. "Where knowledge of your brand resides: The Pareto Share of brand knowledge" Report 44 for Corporate Members (May 2008), Ehrenberg-Bass Institute for Marketing Science.

ROTHSCHILD, M.L.; HYUN, Y.J. "Predicting memory for components of TV commercials from EEG". *Journal of consumer research.* Vol. 16 (1990), No. 4, p. 472-478.

ROTHSCHILD, M.L. [et al.]. "EEG activity and the processing of television commercials". *Communication Research.* Vol. 13 (1986), No. 2, p. 182-220.

SHARP, B. "How brands compete". Report 39 for Corporate Members (2006), Ehrenberg-Bass Institute for Marketing Science.

SIEFERT, C. [et al.]. "Biometric and eye-tracking insights into the efficiency of information processing of television advertising during fast-forward viewing". *International Journal of Advertising.* Vol. 27 (2008), No.3, p. 293-303.

SILBERSTEIN, R.B. "The steady state visually evoked potential as a window into brain functional connectivity associated with cognition". *International Journal of Psychophysiology.* Vol. 61 (2006), No. 3, p. 317-317.

SILBERSTEIN, R.B.; NIELD, G.E. "Brain activity correlates of consumer brand choice shift associated with television advertising", *International Journal of Advertising.* Vol. 27 (2008), No. 3, p. 359-380.

SQUIRE, L.R. "Memory and the Hippocampus: A Synthesis from findings with rats, monkeys and humans". *Psychological Review.* Vol. 99 (1992), No. 2, p. 195-231.

SOLTANI, M.; KNIGHT, R.T. "Neural origins of the P300". *Critical Reviews in Neurobiology.* Vol. 14 (2000), No. 3-4, p. 199-204.

SRULL, T.K. "Affect and memory: the impact of affective reactions in advertising on the representation of product information in memory". *Advances in Consumer Research.* Vol. 10 (1983), No. 1, p. 520-524.

VAKTRATSAS, D.; AMBLER, T. "How advertising works: what do we really know". *Journal of Marketing.* Vol. 63 (2009), p. 26-43.

VAUGH, R. "How advertising works: a planning model revisited". *Journal of Advertising Research.* Vol. 20 (1980), p. 27-33.

WEINSTEIN, S.; APPLE, V.; WEINSTEIN, C. "Brain activity responses to magazine and television advertising". *Journal of Advertising Research.* Vol. 20 (1980), p. 57-63.

THE MAN FROM ZARA
The story of the genius behind the Inditex group
ISBN: 9781907794209

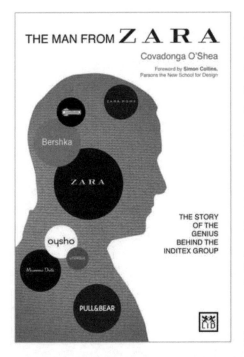

"In this book Covadonga O'Shea delves into the origins of Zara, how the company evolved into the global fashion player we know today and crucially, how it still manages to react so quickly to trends around the world."

Simon Collins, Dean, School of Fashion. Parsons the New School for Design.

Inditex – the group behind Zara, Massimo Dutti, Oysho, Bershka – is today a major force in the world of high-street fashion. It recently outranked Gap as the No.1 clothes retailer in the world. In virtually every city in the world, you will see one or more of Inditex's shops – Zara being the most conspicuous.

Yet little is known about this amazing success. This book offers such an insight by telling the story of the genius behind the Inditex Group – *Armancio Ortega.* Besides being one of the world's richest men, Ortega is the brains behind a modern-day revolution in textiles and fashion retail. Who really is Armancio Ortega? Where is he from? Where is he going? What led him to dream up this empire? Through unprecedented access to Ortega and his closest aides, the author provides a compelling and unique biography of the man responsible for one of this century's most extraordinary business successes.

BEYOND
THE WRITTEN WORD

Authors who speak to you face to face.

Discover LID Speakers, a service that enables businesses to have direct and interactive contact with the best ideas brought to their own sector by the most outstanding creators of business thinking.

- **A network specialising in business speakers, making it easy to find the most suitable candidates.**

- **A website with full details and videos, so you know exactly who you're hiring.**

- **A forum packed with ideas and suggestions about the most interesting and cutting-edge issues.**

- **A place where you can make direct contact with the best in international speakers.**

- **The only speakers' bureau backed up by the expertise of an established business book publisher.**

LIDspeakers.com

Sure value.